SUCCESSFUL FAMILY AND RECREATION ROOMS

SUCCESSFUL FAMILY AND RECREATION ROOMS

Jane Cornell

Structures Publishing Co. 1977
Farmington, Mich.

Manufactured in the United States of America

Edited by Shirley Horowitz

Cover photo courtesy of Georgia-Pacific Corporation

Designed by Patrick Mullaly

Current Printing (last digit)
10   9   8   7   6   5   4   3   2

Library of Congress Cataloging in Publication Data

Cornell, Jane.
    Successful family and recreation rooms.

    Includes index.
    1. Recreation rooms. I. Title
TH3000.C67   690'.8   77-719
ISBN 0-912336-42-0
ISBN 0-912336-439 pbk.

TABLE OF CONTENTS

1. Introducing... The Family/Recreation Room

There are as many reasons for wanting new or updated family/recreation rooms as there are families. Your reasons will dictate the furnishing, color schemes, finishing details, and all the special components needed to individualize your family room. Perhaps you want a room for teen-age jam sessions, complete with accompaniment on guitar and base fiddle. Or a more sedate, away-from-all-the-cares-of-the-world retreat might be your dream. Whatever your goal, you can make your family room whatever you wish. Just take the time to plot and plan it from the very beginning.

The motives for a family room reflect different needs and lifestyles: often-cited is the need for space for a growing family, because more children require more play area. The same area can be cleverly converted into adult recreation space once children are in bed. And the need for play space seems to expand as children approach adulthood.

Family rooms are also a response to today's casual lifestyle. Many homeowners have no intentions of giving up the elegance of their living room for formal entertaining and relaxing. However, they definitely need a special place for easygoing entertaining and congregating. If yours is a family that invariably finds itself ranged around the casual kitchen table, while the formal living room goes uninhabited, it makes good sense to plan an entire room to cope with leisure moments.

A shift of favorite activities and hobbies to your own house is another reason for opting for a family room. Often, new hobbies and interests demand space, and the kind of surroundings at home that can take abuse without showing it. For instance, budding indoor gardeners need space to water and re-pot plants, require no-nonsense surfaces on floors, and counters that will shed water and potting soil. Or, rising teen-age rock stars need space to practice with their bands, with furniture that takes as kindly to sprawling as upright sitting. Easily cleaned surfaces are important here also.

Although your interest in adding a room may be purely for the enjoyment of it, it's nice to know that family room additions are often sound economic choices. One excursion into the market for a new, larger house will convince you of the advantages of working with what you have. Chances are that you can add to your own for a fraction of the cost of purchasing a house with a family room. And, consider the added savings of not having to move at all, in terms of closings, moving fees, and such. Your present home's resale value can also be expected to increase, due to the effort and thought you've put into remodeling. In most homes, the space you need for your family room is right at hand. It may be hidden in an unused, unfinished basement, or a garage, an attic, or an easily enclosed and converted porch. If available, the attic or basement is usually the most logical and economical area for conversion.

No matter where it is located, you will want to make your family/recreation room the best possible space for you and your family. While the temptation may be to go full tilt ahead on such an exciting scheme, this book will give you invaluable tips for assuring your successful plans. Every chapter is designed to cover specific aspects of good family room planning, and execution.

What this Book Covers

Taking first things first, included are guidelines for sizing up your home so that any changes made are the best possible ones. Only by analyzing the entire space available can you most effectively decide which areas should be converted into the all-important family room. It is at this stage that you should decide whether to use a contractor or decorator, or to do it yourself.

Once you have decided on a location, plot the arrangements within the space itself. The mysteries of good furniture placement are easily revealed with floor plans, attention to traffic patterns, and other techniques used by professional interior designers.

Many new materials have been introduced within recent years that make the nuts and bolts business of preparing a family room easier than ever before. New insulation materials can make walls practically noise-proof, as well as keeping heat bills to a minimum. Plumbing, with the new plastic materials available, makes the addition of a family room, cooking center, or powder room reasonable. There are specialty ventilating, dehumidifying, and heating units for every conceivable location. And now you can install the perfect lighting for every hobby, with additional dashes of dramatic lighting for the family room's more general uses.

What could be more romantic and soul-satisfying than a warm and welcoming, crackly fireplace? If your house does not have a built-in fireplace, you can add one economically by using the traditional Franklin stoves or contemporary, free-standing models. Your family room easily can be the decorative showplace in your house. The furnishings and the color scheme you choose will be the most personal touches you will put into this area to bring it all together. While the color possibilities are vast, and furniture styles for family rooms abound, you can put together a compatible, effective mix using the guidelines offered here.

To keep costs to a minimum, try finishing off the walls, floor and ceiling by yourself. Paneling, painting, and papering take a bit of craftsmanship, but are easy to do with the simple instructions included here. With the wide range of decorative effects possible with the new materials, such as heavily textured panels and easily applied scrubbable wall coverings, you have unlimited choice in creating exactly what you want.

Artful disguises for permanent but unpretty elements are suggested at the end of the book. These tricks allow you to hide sinks, work rooms, supports, or pipes. Paint is the least expensive camouflage, while elegant partitions can make entire work areas seem to disappear.

Built-ins are good disguises for other necessary elements, such as laundry centers. They also add a sense of permanence and convenience; you can custom design storage areas to accommodate each and every article needed for hobbies and games. Simple seating can double for storage as well. Ideas for these and other built-ins are covered in detail.

How to Use this Book

The only way for a family room to be successful is for it to reflect the interests and personality of you and your family. So, even if you plan to eventually turn the entire job of creating the family room over to a contractor or interior decorator, it is important that you give as much of yourself to the conception of the room as possible. This book will help you work most efficiently and knowledgeably with whatever outside services you might want to employ.

By doing part of the work or all of it yourself, you will discover the invaluable bonus of creating exactly what you want while cutting a great deal of expense. Reading the entire book, or at least scanning it from start to finish, will give you an overview to keep in mind throughout the development of your family room. And, you will find that many of the suggestions and approaches easily can be applied to other areas of your home as well. When you reach the pertinent stages in your family room's progress, specific chapters will become working guides. Examples are the sections on built-ins, on installing ceilings, or wall coverings.

Because your family room is the one room in the house that must keep up with your family's expanding and growing interests, chances are that you will use this book as your needs demand, in future years.

2. Defining Your Needs

Thinking about the comfort and convenience of a new family or recreation room is enough to give you a warm glow. Many of the problems in your current living environment will disappear with the addition of such a room; but, making that dream a reality means coming to grips with some very down-to-earth facts.

These practical matters should be considered right from the beginning. For instance, you will need to assess honestly exactly what the new area will be used for, both right now and in ensuing years. You must also decide how to best integrate the room with the other areas of your home. In the long run, perhaps a qualified interior decorator or contractor will save you both aggravation and money. And speaking of money, the bottom line on this project may call for financing, so you will want to explore the options available for extra cash.

The following guidelines are especially useful for anyone planning a new family/recreation room. However, they are also useful for anyone updating the family room he already has.

Using the Family Room Space

The family room, more than almost any other area in your home, must cater to all the varied interests of your family. One good way to come to grips with your total needs is to literally sit down and list them. Each family member, from smallest to tallest, can and should join in this activity.

The kinds of criteria you will uncover with such a listing will quickly reveal whether or not you are all thinking on the same wave length. Then you can start establishing the priorities most agreeable to all family members, and use this as the nucleus of your planning.

Most people agree that a family room should be relaxed, so that neither children nor adults feel they must be on good behavior. Start your list with this requirement, but then redefine it to make sure that you all understand what exactly is meant by "relaxed." To teenagers the term may mean noisy rough-housing, and incredible decibels of favorite music. What's "relaxing" to them may be utterly nerve-shattering to someone else.

Then, you can divide this working list into current needs and qualities for special interests, and long-range goals for the space.

Current Needs

Further separate this into "definite musts" and "nice extras." Your own lifestyle will determine which category suits the items on your list. Falling into these general categories would be:

- Inclusion of a powder room

- Ability to close off the area for use as a guest room

- Easy access from the kitchen for play supervision

- Soundproofing so that other areas remain quiet

- Ability to close off the space and not heat it (and conserve energy).

In addition to the many general needs of the family/recreation room, your specific hobbies and interests should figure into your plans. Here are some of the special interests that are often key factors in design.

Creating a party room. Good flooring for dancing, and space to do it, are two considerations for a room that's used mostly for parties. Seating should be comfortable, and be able to accommodate a crowd. But too much seating in large family rooms is intimidating between parties. A good alternative is to have storage areas where extra tables and chairs can be kept out of sight between parties. Movable seating also allows you to arrange the seating to suit whatever activity you plan, from dancing, to a bridge tournament, to home movies.

A second, smaller compact kitchen can save steps and make parties much more fun, if you really plan to entertain a lot. These can vary all the way from actual cooking centers to simple reheating units that keep foods pleasantly warm throughout the party. Include beverage service facilities in your serving plans, too.

Highly polished bare floors and easily moved furniture enable quick conversion of this room for dancing. To counter the harshness of the bare floor, rugs are used decoratively for pillows and on walls, and furniture adds textural interest. (Wicker furniture from Chromcraft)

Lighting can make or break a party, so make sure that the lighting system you install enhances the party mood. Lighting is especially important in basement party rooms that have little natural light. Plan your lighting so that it can be used atmospherically for a party, but also altered to make an empty party room seem warm, cosy, and useful.

A good sound system is important to any party, whether background country music or chamber music. Other electrical accoutrements might include a large television for Saturday afternoon ball-game watching. Or, consider a movie projector opposite a wall that can accommodate a screen.

Access to the outdoors from the family room expands your party-giving area. If outdoor entertaining is part of your family fun, then consider arranging your room so that it can serve as home base for the barbecue cook. For instance, you might install a second kitchen area near the outer door, rather than putting it near an interior wall.

Planning a playroom. Many of the qualities of a good party room are also ideal for a playroom. Among

When your family/recreation room is really a playroom, why not go all out and decorate it for kids? A nautical theme sets the tone for this red, white, and blue room, with storage, sleeping, and hiding spaces built right in. Anso nylon carpet warms it up. (Allied Chemical Corp.)

these are: open space with cleared, cleanable flooring for messy games; storage for a multitude of toys; and, a good serving center, where children can help themselves without interfering with meal-making. Carefree surfaces on all walls, floors and furniture make the most sense. "Childproof" materials are available in all three categories, thanks to some of the new synthetics. Today, even carpeting is sufficiently easy-to-clean so that the harsh, bare floors of most past playrooms are no longer necessary.

A separate entrance to the outdoors, with an ample setup for removing outer garments and galoshes, and promptly putting them away, can make a playroom double as a mudroom. With younger ones, an extra shower in the family room not only eases normal bathroom congestion, but enables cleanup before anyone can track dirt through the rest of the house.

Safety absolutely should be the major criteria for any of the materials in a playroom. Avoid any jutting edges on walls, built-ins, or furniture. Make sure that any electrical wires are out of the way, and insulated. Choose skid-resistant flooring and avoid loose scatter rugs. Assume that you will design the room so invitingly that the children will want to play freely in it. Assume, too, that when they are playing, children may throw caution to the wind, so it is your duty to make the environment as safe as possible.

Extra sturdy furniture for a playroom should be comfortable for both grownups and children alike. Stationary pieces should be relatively tip-proof. Keep in mind that the overstuffed, casual furniture pieces that are extremely comfortable for a sprawling adult are often simply overscaled for children. One common offender is the proverbial built-in couch. If your youngsters have not achieved full growth yet, set couches low, and provide extra-deep back pillows to support smaller bodies. No one sits comfortably when his back does not reach the back of the couch, or feet do not touch the floor.

Of course, adult-scaled furniture should be included also, because all generations will want to use the room. The bean-bag chairs that have become so popular recently can serve both children and adults. Balance the furnishings between those that are best for small folks, and those that suit grownups.

Catering to special interests. More and more people are investing their leisure hours in hobbies and crafts that could properly be called avocations. If your family has taken up one or more interests, then the family room may be the logical center to pursue these activities. It is, in the truest sense, a recreation room when the favorite activities of the clan are centralized in that space.

Some of the activity areas that call for special interior planning include music centers, art and craft cen-

ters, workshops, photography centers, home movie centers, sewing or quilting areas, indoor gardening areas and guests rooms.*

Music centers should be planned from the walls in. Good acoustical surfaces on ceilings, walls and even the floor, will make music enjoyment all the greater. The true afficionado may want to plan the sound system first, and then build the seating arrangement

The stair wall provides step-up home office space, while a storage counter wall hides a multitude of hobby and sewing accessories. The printed Anso nylon carpet carries the pattern needed to unify the room, which was designed by Virginia Frankel. (Allied Chemical Corp.)

Old-shoe, soft simulated-leather beanbag chairs are ideal for this music listening area. They encourage lounging and casual entertaining, which is just the mood wanted by most family rooms. ("Old Shoe" beanbag chairs and ottomans by Decorion)

*Specific layouts, equipment, lighting and spatial treatments for each activity center can be found in *Successful Studios and Work Centers* by Margaret Davidson.

around it, to get best location for the sound. Consider a good storage system, where one can catalogue and keep dust from tapes or records until ready to use.

If playing rather than listening is the main activity, then take a tip from the music rooms of the past and provide a suitable performing area. A fledgling rock and roll band would be thrilled with a raised platform at one end of the room, lighting that could simulate a professional theater, and plenty of extra chairs for guests.

Adequate electrical outlets are very important for today's modern instruments, such as electric guitars. So, start with an assessment of the instruments you play, plus the occasional ones brought in by friends, and then allow an extra electrical load for newly discovered instruments. There is nothing more frustrating than a jam session that is aborted because fuses are blown. An additional electrical line might be a necessity rather than a luxury for your kind of music.

Painting or crafting centers call primarily for good lighting, floors and furnishings that will resist spills, and a water source somewhere nearby. If a true north light is not possible, consider installation of fluorescent lighting that will substitute for it. Good lighting and the right furnishings are essential to lessen fatigue, especially when engrossed with a hobby. Make sure that looms, drawing boards, or easels and their corresponding seats are the most comfortable height. Remember to plan display and storage areas for the finished creative projects.

Workshops, according to many safety experts, should be enclosed so that they may be locked, especially if there are dangerous machines and small children who might want to imitate the worker. Good lighting is more a safety factor here than just aesthetics. So is good ventilation, since many workshop projects produce harmful by-products such as fine sawdust, re-finishing fumes, and paint fumes.

There are almost as many storage systems as there are workshop owners, for most are uniquely geared to the specific needs of any hobby. Make your first workshop project a good orderly system of storage, to protect expensive tools and parts and prevent frustration.

A photography workshop can be as complicated or compact as you need. Keep in mind that an enclosed darkroom can be almost any shape, so that your thinking need not be limited to a box-like enclosure in a corner. For instance, you might align your darkroom equipment along one long wall and close off that entire end of the room, making the original room shorter.

Home movie recreation rooms put the greatest stress on well-planned seating arrangements. The seating should allow for a walk space behind the projector as well as a comfortable view of the screen.

Modular seating units, comfortably upholstered and in mix-match shapes (armless, with side arms, with foot stools, etc.), can be arranged at will to convert a conversational seating arrangement into an opulent theatre. Make sure that you combine seating with occasional tables. They can be used for drinks during home shows, and easily moved into other positions when the room is meant for just talking. Light control can be as simple as using backed draperies or opaque shades, or as lavish as some of the newer blinds with their distinctly Hollywood feeling.

A sewing center calls for lots of storage for ready-to-use fabrics, as well as a good working center. If you are constantly involved with sewing projects, then a permanent work space makes more sense than a fold-up hideaway arrangement. Include a comfortable table for cutting as well as sewing. Locating a sewing center near the laundry area makes it easy for you to make necessary little repairs discovered at the last minute. Occasional sewers can combine activities by arranging their sewing notions in storage units near an expansive table normally used for games or eating.

An indoor gardening center calls for a water source, which may be an updated, conventional basement laundry sink. Like other somewhat messy hobbies, the perfect surroundings for indoor gardening are those that require least fuss and are easy to clean. Keep in mind that you will want to have desk space and book shelf space, as well as planting space. If most of your indoor plants are destined for the outdoors, consider placing this area near the outer door. And, while you are at it, investigate some of the prefabricated greenhouse additions that are abundant in the market (see Suppliers list).

Family guest rooms take special planning. In many cases, an extra bath and kitchen facilities in this miniature living unit afford the guest a sense of having a special place all his own, without being a burden to the hostess or rest of the family. Comfortable sleeping accommodations are easily hidden in convertible sofas during the day, or in built-in bedding units. However, keep in mind that any bed that opens out requires extra space. Make sure furniture such as a coffee table can be easily moved at night. Plan your lighting so that a bedside lamp is easy to reach, and include night lights for guest safety. Arrange some way of closing off the space when it is inhabited. Even with a large opening to the rest of the home, you can give a guest a measure of privacy with a temporary sliding screen partition that can be shifted back when not in use.

Multi-Purpose and Long-Range Uses

These are factors to be considered before you order the first bag of nails. Unless your family is firmly committed to special interests, you will want a family room that can be versatile enough for use both now and for years to come.

To allow longevity, confine any decorative touches that might date the room to easily removed features. For instance, if you want a nautical theme, incorporate it into the upholstery fabric or drapery fabric and wall accents, rather than building a design into a permanent floor. The temptation to incorporate design themes seems especially strong when decorating for children or teenagers, but locking a room into any permanent theme for younger ages is particularly chancey. Children resent rooms they feel are childish, and they can outgrow "cute" decorations very quickly.

Multi-purpose doubleups are particularly handy in coping with a small space. For instance, a kitchenette with a pass-through for easy patio dining can double as a planting center. A raised platform for a teen rock band's performances can easily become the center stage for home movie viewing. Matching square Parsons tables, used for bridge or chess, can be grouped together for a good sized sewing table. With ample storage for cumbersome toys, a children's playroom with wide space in the center can be used for square dancing and other adult activities.

Two-stage planning now will enable you to convert your family room to future activities with less trouble. You can thus avoid a complete remodeling later, and the corresponding costs. Here are some examples of two-stage thinking that will help the family/recreation room grow with your family.

- Plan a snack center for youngsters that also can serve as a teen and adult beverage counter.

- Design a large toy storage area that will easily convert into the darkroom an amateur photographer has always wanted.

- Put the no-fuss, damage-proof flooring for the children's arts and crafts area near adequate natural lighting so that it later becomes an ideal adult artist's space.

- Use more formal, neutral wall coverings and decorative accents if the room is eventually to be converted into a bedroom, and make sure that the room can be completely closed off for privacy.

What Total House Plan Makes the Most Sense?

No addition to your home can be considered in a vacuum. Whether you are planning to add a new room or merely to convert unused space, the way in which the family room works with the rest of your home is of prime importance. To make the most workable arrangement for your entire home, you may want to change the functions of some of the existing spaces.

To begin your total house plan analysis, define the current functions of the rooms now used. List each room, what its primary function is, and the other activities that are now centered in it. For instance, your master bedroom might now function primarily for sleeping. Secondary functions might include a home office, and a sewing center. You may not need as much space for your master bedroom, if those secondary functions were shifted somewhere else.

Include the aesthetics to be considered with each room as well. If the view of the yard from your bedroom window sets up your entire day, you will want to keep the bedroom location. On the other hand, reassigning your rooms might help solve some existing problems. If your bedroom is unpleasantly unprivate, and constantly shuttered because it is too close to the neighbors or too near the kitchen's constant noise, a change to another bedroom might be desirable.

List possible expansions or conversions of unused spaces to give yourself a total look at your home's possibilities. Of course, you may have only one clear-cut choice for expansion. However, make sure that you have not overlooked some of the more usual areas that are chosen for family room remodeling. These include the basement, attic, porch, and garage. Add to these the unused or poorly used areas in your home. These might include an over-large front foyer, a pantry, or general utility room. Another area might be a seldom-used guest or catch-all room.

Try different room assignments on paper, giving full reign to your most creative thoughts on use of space. Often, it is just this ability to organize space that makes the work of professional remodelers and interior decorators so successful. Try all the alternatives until you settle on the best one for your particular needs.

For instance, the obvious room for expansion in your home may be to finish off an unused attic. Perhaps this is where your family room should be located for quiet activities. However, if workshop or laundry area needs must be filled by the family room, it might be better to convert another room. Then you can finish the attic to take over the old room's function. Consider that, while unsuitable for a family room, the attic might be ideal for a welcome master bedroom retreat. The old master bedroom, if located near the kitchen, might be a good location for your new family room.

Could that unused dining room become a child's bedroom? How about making the unfinished attic a children's dormitory? Should your existing living room become the family party room, while the sun-porch becomes a smaller, more formal, "adult" living room? You probably have more possibilities in your home than you imagined.

In assessing a room's adaptability to another function, consider some of these factors:

• The position of the room and its windows for privacy. This is most important in considering the rearrangement of bedrooms.

• Proximity to a bathroom or the kitchen. Obviously, you can't arbitrarily put the dining room across the house from the kitchen. Nor would you want a young child's room far from a bath.

• Availability of plumbing, wiring, and other essentials for a specific function. While most of these can be added to any area of the home, often it would be far less expensive to add a second kitchen or other major element in one area than it would be in another.

• Nearness to the outdoors. A family room for a family who practically spends all of its time outdoors would be most convenient with a separate entrance directly outside.

• Cost of heating, insulation, and advantages of closing off the area for heat-saving. With fuel costs increasing yearly, you may well want to close off and lower the heating of rooms that are not used frequently, or some bedrooms.

• Ease of access. A room that you use frequently should not be tucked way up in the attic for most efficiency. However, children might love the adventure of a flight of stairs up to their own bedroom.

• How your family room will work for parties, if it is to be the main entertaining area. Since most parties overflow to the rest of the house, consider the problems of getting food to the family room; how easy will it be to move from that room to the rest of the house; and whether your guests will have to invade the privacy of other rooms you would prefer to have off limits.

• Costs of converting more than one room versus your budget and long-range livability of the plan. To make your house function really efficiently, expenses in rearranging the rooms in the beginning may well be justified. A poorly located and inte- grated family room will not only be less enjoyable, it will not add appreciably to the value of your home.

Will You Need a Professional's Services?

If you truly love working on your home, and have some experience in that area, then let yourself do everything. Be realistic, however; if you really loathe or do not have the knowledge to handle such tasks as wiring, plumbing, or even painting, then call on the professionals. The best way to destroy any home improvement plan is to be unrealistic about how much you are really going to actually do yourself.

Professionals often are able to work out ways of splitting the workload, so that they handle what you want to farm out, and leave the rest to you. It does not have to be an all-or-nothing situation, but one in which you can arrange the fees and aid to best suit your budget and work needs.

Having a firm idea before beginning is one way to save costs. That is why clearly determining the kind of room and the functions that are to take place within it is the first step, whether you plan to do most of the job yourself, or to use outside help.

It may even be penny-wise and pound-foolish to attempt to do the job without at least a consultation with a professional. He can make sure that your plans comply with existing building codes, and can file whatever permits are necessary.

What Type of Professional?

The three main professions that are most involved with recreation rooms are home remodeling contractors, architects, and interior designers. You may want the services of one of these, or even all three, to finish your family room. Only you can judge the amount of work that you can plan for yourself, and comfortably take on without outside aid.

Architects. Particularly helpful if you want to rearrange existing spaces within your house. He is also a good choice if you will be making structural changes such as enlarging windows or doors, or putting up an entire extension.

Payments are usually based on a percentage of the job, or hourly fees. Generally, architects charge a percentage fee for the full architectural service of taking over an entire job; fees range from 10 to 15 percent. It is possible that the architect's entire fee would be covered by the construction savings he can guide you to.

Another way to work with an architect is to consult with him on an hourly basis, as you might with an attorney. He can give you professional advice, and even provide rough sketches or plans, while you take it from there. You might have him check out your rough plans, and give you advice on such things as materials, colors and the like. The fees that architects charge for such services vary, so be sure you know in advance what to expect.

Finding the right architect is important, too. The American Institute of Architects, an organization of professionals, is one source. They are often listed in the telephone book, and can provide you with names of architects who specialize in house design and improvements. Or, you can contact the National A.I.A. Headquarters at 1735 New York Avenue, N.W., Washington, D.C. 20006.

Another source is friends who have had remodeling done, if you like the end results. Although you may not want to ask them actual costs, you can ask them such leading questions as whether the work was completed on time (with the normal delays that are bound to take place), and whether they found the architect easy to work with. A good leading question is whether the finished job was in line with the original plan. Keep in mind that the architect may not have had total control over the job, and use some judgment in weighing the answers.

See examples of the architect's work before you proceed on your own job with him. Most architects are only too happy to show you pictures of other jobs that are somewhat similar to yours. If his vision is not at all in line with yours (for instance, if almost all of his work has a modern stamp, while you definitely want an Early American feeling in your place), then he may not be the man for you.

One of the most reassuring references for an architect is the satisfaction of his own past clients. If he is handling your entire recreation room project, in many cases he would be happy to take you to see an already-completed job.

Home Improvement Contractor. Just the professional for the job if you have few major structural changes affecting the entire house, but still do not want to handle the entire job yourself. He is often willing to handle only part of the work (such as installing new wiring or plumbing, or creating new walls), and to arrange for materials so you can finish the rest yourself. Today's reputable home improvement contractor is used to handling all types of jobs, and may have interior designers on staff.

Payments to the contractor, and their timing, should be clearly spelled out in a written agreement that covers plans and specifications. As with architects, you often can offset the cost of the contractor through the savings in materials and the assurance that the job will be well done and on time.

Talk to more than one contractor, and compare the estimates given. A bid that is very low may mean that you get very little for your money. You are better off comparing those contractors who are within the same price range, and checking to see that the quality of the materials each specifies is comparable.

Selecting a qualified contractor can begin by a check with the headquarters of the local chapter of the National Home Improvement Council, many of which are located in metropolitan areas. Or, you can write to the national headquarters at 11 East 44th Street, New York, N.Y., 10017. Choosing a member of this Council helps ensure that your contractor is ethical, reliable, and knowledgeable.

The National Home Improvement Council (NHIC) suggests these pointers in selecting a qualified contractor for your job:

1. Employ a contractor with an established place of business, preferably in your locality.

2. Be sure he has adequate financial references.

3. Get references from him of satisfied customers, and check on them personally by phone. Check the Better Business Bureau to see if they have an adverse file on him. If no Bureau branch exists in your community, check with the local Chamber of Commerce.

4. Observe carefully how precisely he "sizes up" your proposed project. Take note of his suggestions and discuss them thoroughly with him, taking time to understand them fully.

5. Be sure to have written agreement on plans and specifications.

6. Have a thorough understanding as to the quality of materials and workmanship required. All materials should be specified in the contract by brand names and quantity.

7. If plans are required, insist that you okay them before work is started. Study the plan carefully.

8. Have all the restrictions for building codes, permits needed, and the fees to be paid spelled out in your contract. These complex details respecting required permits in your area are well-known by a good local contractor, since he works with them every day.

9. Have your contractor provide a Certification of Insurance covering Workmen's Compensation, property damage, and personal liability.

10. Consider the advantages of the contractor cleaning up after the job is finished. Many contracts specify that cleanup of all debris and materials will be done for an additional cost, leaving your place "brush clean." It will save you much work and trouble.

11. In addition to the NHIC suggestions above, you might also want to get in writing the starting and completion dates on the job, and have a copy of the contractor's license number. The timing of each element of the job is one of the major ways in which a professional contractor can excell. He knows how to order and plan things so that they are done in the most efficient order; you will want the job done smoothly and with as little disruption to your home as possible.

Interior Designer. While some, especially the independent ones, have the facility to handle the contracting necessary, their main specialty is in organizing and coordinating the furnishings so that they are both attractive and functional. If your family room will be a showcase, you may want professional help in choosing the furniture, color scheme, and other aesthetic elements.

Many of the pointers in choosing and working with either an architect or a remodeling contractor are good guides in working with an interior designer. One advantage in working with an interior designer is that they often can provide you with unique and exclusive furnishings, sold through decorators only and unavailable in regular retail outlets.

If you plan to purchase furnishings for your family room from one main store, take advantage of the store's own interior design staff. While payment arrangements will vary from designer to designer, you can often work out a practical arrangement with a store to use its design services, providing you buy most of the furnishings from them. The cost of the designer is often in reverse proportion to the amount you spend ...cheapest when you consolidate your purchases with one firm, and use their staff. Some stores offer free design services if you buy their furnishings.

Payments to interior designers can be one-shot consultation fees, a long-term fee covering the stages of the project, or a percentage of the cost of the furnishings and materials that are specified for the job. Professional interior designers will be happy to work with you in making the kind of arrangements that best suit your budget. Be sure, however, that you give designers an honest estimate of what you want to spend right at the beginning, both for the project, and for their part in it. Do not feel you have to have a large budget before using an interior designer.

Select an interior designer by using the general guidelines for a contractor or architect. Membership in the American Society of Interior Designers is one good guide to a designer's proficiency. Check your local phone book for listing of members, or write to the national headquarters of ASID at 730 Fifth Avenue, New York, N.Y. 10019.

Will You Need Financing?

Financing your recreation room remodeling may be worth the extra cost due to time savings for completion. Or, your budget may frankly demand some outside resource.

Include in your financing plans ALL the elements that are necessary to make your family room come to life. You will have estimates for the major jobs, and those to be done by outside help, as a basis. But, don't forget the finishing touches, such as lamps, accessories, rugs, and so forth. There is nothing so discouraging as having the job halfway there...and then being unable to complete it.

When it comes to committing yourself to any payments, either to a professional or to a lending institution, make sure you understand all the elements of a contract before you sign it. In many cases, you will have a three-day "cooling off" period during which you can change your mind, even after signing a contract, and cancel it. If you don't have one in your contract, then give yourself one by being completely sure before you sign anything. The best financial plan is the one you continue to be happy with, after the work is done.

Check your options for this loan as you would for any other kind of monetary transaction. Interest rates vary so much from lending institution to lending institution, and from time to time, that no specific rules will cover every situation. Be prepared to shop around. One good place to start is with your local contractor. He probably already works closely with the established lending institutions in your community, and can even act as the go-between. But, go beyond him, and do some comparison shopping yourself. You will want to compare interest rates and length of time to repay the loan. Be sure that whatever assets you may have are considered, such as a sizable equity in the property to be improved, or another recognized investment. By shopping around, you can find the best financing for your plans and your purse strings.

3. Setting the Mood

While the sound planning that goes into the basics of a good family room design are important for its livability, it's the charisma you bring to it that makes it a success. You set the mood of and put your personal stamp on the room through choice of colors, furniture styles, and the way they are brought into a unified whole.

By exploring your true likes and dislikes in colors and styles, you can develop combinations that will please you for this year, and future years. Color schemes, furniture styles, coordinating patterns, themes, and some of the special furniture pieces particularly suited to family rooms, are all discussed in this chapter.

Color Schemes for the Whole Family

Color is the most important element in a room, according to many interior designers. People will react almost violently to colors they hate, or find their psyche soothed by a color they love. Since color tastes are so strong, it is a good idea to be very sure everyone in your family likes the colors you plan to use for this communal area. A caucus may give you a choice of main colors that are high on everyone's list.

The choice of color available is as broad as the infinite mixtures easily created in a paint can. Finding exact colors is a little more difficult for upholstery, paneling, or flooring, but even in these lines you will find an expanding selection.

You can use color as a cohesive force to unify spaces, to accent special areas, or even to disguise some areas. But, before you venture into the trickery of color, take time to review the basics of color selection and coordination.

The dynamics within each color give it a character all its own. The inherent characteristics of colors can be identified as hue, value or brightness, and saturation or intensity. These are the qualities that give us the infinite variety of colors, and distinguish one from another.

Hue is sometimes used interchangeably with color, to distinguish one part of the color spectrum from another. For instance, red is a different hue than blue or green. You need to know the hue to be able to work out a color scheme according to sound color balancing principles. *Value or brightness* is a measure of the lightness or darkness of a color, from white on one end, to black on the other. *Shades* are colors with a value nearer black, while *tints* are colors with a value nearer white. For instance, with a primary blue, an accent of "baby blue" would be a tint of that color, while "midnight blue" would be a shade. Both come from the same hue, but with varying degrees of lightness or darkness.

Light colors (tints) seem airier than dark colors (shades). Use these properties to advantage when choosing a color scheme. Use light tints to make a room look more spacious, less enclosed; or, for a basement, less weighted down. Use dark shades to make large spaces seem warmer and cosier.

Saturation or intensity refers to the amount of color in pure or unadulterated form. Colors straight from a child's paint-pots are almost always of high intensity. They can be muted through the addition of either white or grey, which cuts down the exact degree of saturation of the pure color. For example, the yellow of a buttercup is saturated and intense, while the softened yellow of sweet peas has less saturation, although basically the same hue.

Intense colors are exuberant, zingy, forceful and often extrovertedly happy. They demand attention as much as intense conversations or people do, so use them sparingly in a color scheme to avoid tiring of them. Muted colors have comforting qualities, pleasantly making their presence known, but without demanding attention. These are the favorite choices for the main color in a color scheme, since they wear well in the long run.

Warmth and coolness are the two other qualities of colors that give them personality. The easiest way to see which category fits a specific color is to look at the color wheel in the color section of this book. Bisect the color wheel on an axis that goes through the yellow/violet. The colors to the right are warm colors: yellow, yellow-orange, orange, red-orange, red, red-violet, violet. The colors on the left are cool colors: yellow, yellow-green, green, green-blue, blue, blue-violet, violet. The two colors that are at the cross-over points (yellow and violet) can appear either warm or cool, depending upon their hue, intensity, value, or relationship to the other colors with which they are used. Warm colors visually tend to come closer, which is a

Natty naturals plus black and white set the color scheme for this sleek family room. Crafted artifacts echo the hand-hewn character of the resilient flooring derived from Early American stencil patterns, laid in tiles although the flooring looks like sheet. (Arlington by Azrock)

This sophisticated family room boasts an easy-care, large-scale ceramic tile floor for quick cleanups. Placed near the kitchen, a supersized table doubles for casual meals, or hobbies, or games. The monochromatic color scheme makes use of textures, such as the bark feeling and chestnut glaze of the tile. (Terra Vitra by American Olean tile)

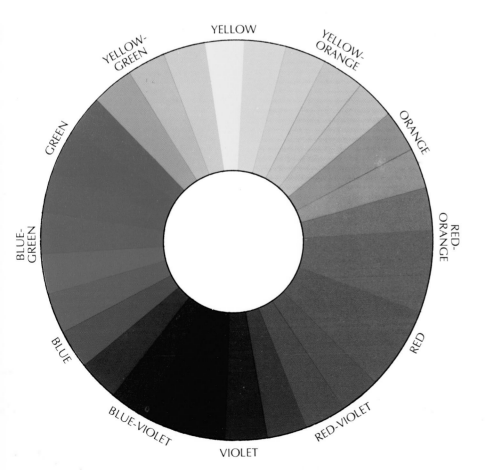

Use this color wheel to help build your own color schemes.

Strong structural beams accent the lines of the soffit and bring out the rich grain of paneling judiciously used in this family room. The weathered wood paneling uses interesting application with horizontal lines. (Oregon Trail paneling, from Georgia-Pacific)

Tough tile flooring gives lightness and brightness to this family room. Diagonal placement of furniture fills the room for family use, but can be pushed back for dancing or play. (Murray quarry tile, "Fawn Gray", by American Olean Tile)

Create your own indoor garden with wicker and lattice moldings on walls and window shutters, splashed with lovely green, yellow, and white. The moldings come from retail building materials outlets. (Photo from the Western Wood Moulding Producers)

◀ Take a carpeting with character and let it carry the room, as done here with comic-strip inspired pattern. Although the carpeting subject is comical, the sophisticated colors chosen by designer Peggy Walker gear the room for adult use. ("Comics" carpet from Bigelow-Sanford, Inc.)

A split level gives architectural interest, especially when set off by red carpeting; the impact makes up for small size. White ABS plastic furniture adds zippy contrast while blue completes the Americana color scheme, designed by Virginia Frankel. (Syroco LifeStyle furniture)

Create a grand entrance such as this one for your family room. It cleverly includes a built-in bar. Note how the rug design leads the eye invitingly to the room beyond. ("North Star" rug by Ege Rya, Inc.)

◀ Use of the country cupboard wall unit makes this family room—otherwise lacking in architectural interest—rich, novel, and exciting. The Early American theme is carried throughout, spiced with bright primary colors by designer Shirley Regendahl. (Sugar Hill furniture, Bigelow-Sanford carpeting)

The sweeping lines of a circular staircase are structurally joined to the window treatment through the use of bright matching paint. The simple shades that regulate light are in keeping with the straight lines of the window wall, by designer Shirley Regendahl. (Window Shade Manufacturers Assn.)

A brick-look floor in vinyl sets off a prized Oriental rug, eclectically mixed with denim-covered sofa and chairs. The color scheme is a variation of primaries, red, blue and yellow. ("Bricktone" Vinyl Corlon by Armstrong)

Area rugs set off the game/dining table and conversational area in this family room. Lightly scaled furniture keeps the room from becoming too crowded, has easily cleaned chrome frames, and can be rearranged at will for dancing. (James David Furniture, Ege Rya Rugs)

Up the wall goes the flooring to coordinate this stair landing entrance; wood parquet floor tile is repeated behind books in the bookcase. Vinyl tiles like these are easy to install and attractive almost anywhere. ("Concord Woods" tile from Azrock Floor Products)

An outer corner fireplace gives a good view of the hearth from two angles, including the conveniently arranged seating section. Note that shades adjust from both top and bottom for full control, and provide a handsome background. (Designed by Virginia Frankel for Syroco furniture)

Use the attic if you have no other space for a family room; you can still have effective results. Smart panels make the most of angled roof lines, while a sofa and Hide-A-Bed quickly convert the room for overnight guests. ("Suffolk" furniture styles by Simmons)

A smart and dashing wall covering treatment gives all the design impact this room needs. Modular seating in a cosy corduroy can be rearranged at will, while light carpeting adds spaciousness. (Imperial Wallcoverings and Collins & Aikmen Carpeting)

Wicker and chrome combined with white and blue give a wonderfully Southwestern feeling to this family room. As cool as a seascape, the room works well for parties but keeps its comfortable, serene air. (Chromcraft furniture)

Those sophisticated chairs are actually recliners, a good example of how to combine convenience and good looks. The bunching tables serve as a coffee table, but are easily positioned as side tables wherever needed. (Barcalounger Recliners and Peters-Revington bunching tables)

You do not have to have an Early American house to have a traditional family room. Stucco overhead beams, paneling and homespun fabrics, and warm accessories set the tone. Recliners serve for lounging or handwork, with good lighting right at hand. Note the effective repeat of line in pillows and hanging baskets. (Barcalounger Recliners)

Everything right at hand and all in order for this functional family room. A multitude of hobbies can be organized with open storage such as this. Colorful carpeting acts as the unifying agent; it is actually easily installed carpet tiles. (Armstrong Handi-stick "Harvest Spice" tiles)

Wall systems such as these are ideal for creating a focus wall and giving storage at the same time. You can choose enclosed or open modules to suit your own needs. Elegant furniture such as this balances the heft of the wall unit. (Founders furniture and wall system in Patterns 30, Armstrong "Oakwynne" carpeting)

Designer, Ms. Michael Love, used a sophisticated hexagon floor tile in three colors to give this room excitement. Bi-fold doors are ready-made, painted a sharp color and used to close off a children's area when wanted. Textured white paneling keeps basement room airy. (Champion Building Products, U.S. Plywood)

A small card-playing table tucks into the bookcase corner when not in use, to give full view of either the fireplace or window. Vertical blinds give the window a modern look, and provide window more importance than some treatments would. (Photo courtesy Window Shade Manufacturers Assn.)

A colorfully painted cabinet wall holds all the accessories needed for indoor gardening. Although the units are free-standing, they have a built-in look. Alternating white and yellow sections make it easy to remember what is stored in each area. (Ethan Allen furniture)

Gourmets can store extra cooking aids in the surrounding cabinet units in this family room/kitchen combination. Straw-look baskets and a natural fiber rug make cohesive secondary accessories for country Americana furniture. (Furniture by Ethan Allen)

This family/recreation room is formal enough for any kind of entertaining. Side sofa is shifted in summer to face the view, reversing the seating arrangement. (Ethan Allen Furniture)

property you can use to decorative advantage. For instance, you might make a large family room seem more intimate by painting an accent wall a bright tomato red. Cool colors tend to recede. You can exploit this property by choosing a cool color scheme (perhaps blue and green) for a small space such as a powder room.

Basic color relationships form the classic color schemes that are the mainstay of the decorator. Colors are divided into groupings according to their position on the color wheel. The four main color groupings are primaries, secondary colors, intermediate or tertiary colors, and the neutrals.

Primary colors are pure colors that cannot be produced by mixing other colors. The primaries are yellow, red, and blue. This big three forms the basis for all of the other colors in the spectrum.

Secondary colors are produced by combining equal parts of two of the primaries. They are orange, violet, and green. They fall half-way between the primaries on the color wheel. Equal parts of yellow and red produce orange. Equal parts of red and blue give violet. Equal parts of blue and yellow create green.

Tertiary colors are produced by mixing equal parts of a primary color and its closest secondary color. They are yellow-orange, orange-red, red-violet, violet-blue, blue-green, green-yellow.

While more fanciful names are given to colors, especially the tertiary colors, it often helps in working out a color scheme to remember which grouping they belong to and identify them that way.

Neutrals are non-colors, and are composed of those tones from white to black, and all tones of grey. Not-quite neutrals include the colors in the beige and brown-black family, since they can have relatively little effect on the true colors in a color scheme. Almost every color scheme benefits from the use of neutrals. White gives freshness and spaciousness, while black gives a dramatic underscoring to a color scheme. A totally neutral scheme, with perhaps mere hints of true color, is a very sophisticated and somewhat austere way of decorating.

Specific color schemes have been developed through the years along the lines of the most pleasing combinations for colors. Although anyone can use whatever colors preferred, these relationships and the understanding of them help in achieving a successful result.

Color Schemes

Once you have chosen the favorite basic color for your room, look through these possible combinations to see which would work best for you.

The Monochromatic Scheme. Many shades of a single color are used, simple and attractive for small spaces, since it tends to unify and expand at the same time. Walls might be pale blue, woodwork and carpeting a medium shade of blue, with jaunty nautical accents in bright royal blue. In order to avoid possible monotony, use white and black accents and a variation of textures.

The Analogous Scheme. Colors adjoining each other on the color wheel such as yellow, plus avocado plus green, or red plus terra cotta plus orange. Next to monochromatic schemes, these are the easiest to use, and allow you to flaunt your favorite colors. The colors usually are not in their pure form, but instead are used in varying values and intensities, with one color dominating.

The Analogous Scheme plus a complementary accent. Similar to the above, with the addition of an accent color that is directly opposite on the color wheel. An example would be a yellow-green, green, and blue-green color scheme with accents of red. This scheme livens up a large area, where a totally analogous scheme might become boring.

The Complementary Scheme. A combination of two colors opposite each other on the color wheel; for example, blue-and-orange, yellow-and-violet, and red-and-green. Each color makes the other look more attractive, and when mixed together, they give a neutral gray, which indicates perfect balance.

The Near or Split Complementary Scheme. Takes the form of a "Y" on the color wheel, drawing one color from one side, and splitting the color choice on the other. An example would be a yellow-orange, red-orange split combined with a blue. It differs from an analogous scheme with a complementary color in that the central color is not used (in this case, orange itself).

The Double-Split Complementary Scheme. Takes the form of an "X" on the color wheel. This sophisticated scheme demands a good color sense to pull it off successfully, so that the elements look cohesive. It is a good choice for a large space, since such schemes are often interesting and lively. To vary the scheme above and make it a double-split, the colors used would be yellow-orange and red-orange, plus blue-green and blue-violet.

The Triadic Scheme. Combines the three colors located on three equal points of the wheel, such as the primaries (yellow, red, blue), or secondaries (orange, violet, green). Variations in the intensities of the hues, values, and tones are what make this scheme work well. The addition of gold or yellow to a traditional red, white, and blue Americana scheme makes it triadic, and brings the individual colors into better focus.

Basic brown of paneling is balanced with light wicker and sofas in reds and ochre, echoed in the rug. Armless furniture lightens up the heft of the paneling and matching wood storage units. Sofas are really hide-a-beds. ("Avanti" furniture by Simmons)

Creating your own scheme starts by deciding on the main color, then working up possible combinations that will both please your sensibilities and best work with space at hand. Much as you might love warm, dark colors, they can make a small family room look far too claustrophobic if used in quantity. So consider using a light, airy tint for the main tones, and go wild with an accent wall or throw in pillows in whatever bright colors you choose.

Paint stores are the perfect place to develop your own personal pallette. Color chips are ideal for deciding on a color combination: through mixing and matching, trial and error, you will develop the general color scheme. Chances are that it will follow one of the schemes outlined here. Once you have chosen it, then you can assign the relative amounts of each color you want. A good rule of thumb is to make the larger wall surfaces a muted color and the major furniture pieces subdued; then introduce accent colors in small doses.

Remember that paneling is a color, too! Browns are actually shades of deep orange, and must be figured into any color scheme, since they affect it. See if you can get a folder that illustrates the paneling of your choice so you can work it into your initial color scheme plans. It will save you many headaches later on if you have incorporated the paneling into your color scheme thinking.

To incorporate wood-toned paneling into your color scheme, work out its relationships, keeping in mind that it is an orange hue. For instance, the complementary color is blue. That's why blue and white are so stunning against warm woodgrain. The triadic matchmates are lavender and green. Close analagous neighbors of brown are yellow-orange and red-orange.

In assembling your color scheme, use the paint chips, swatches of fabrics, and paneling samples. Once you have decided on a scheme, make up a page or folder in which your color choices are clearly identified, along with samples of each color. By having a record, you will be able to duplicate a color exactly, should you want to touch it up. When you want to change part of the scheme in later years, you can use your original samples to find other compatible coordinates.

Here are some pointers in choosing the colors for a family room.

• For northern exposures and cool rooms, consider warm hues that will give the room visual warmth, such as reds, oranges, or yellows.

• For southern exposures and sunny hot rooms, consider cool hues that will give a room spaciousness and a sense of coolness, such as blues and greens.

• For low-ceilinged rooms, try white or a light color tint to visually raise the roof.

• For high-ceilinged rooms, try a tint slightly darker than the walls.

• Color unsightly objects the same color as their backgrounds to help them disappear. This is most effective in muted tones. Use this technique to disguise exposed pipes or awkward areas that can't be structurally changed.

• Suit the vitality of the colors you use to the activities of the room. A family room for resting and hobbies might need a toned-down color scheme. On the other hand, a room where you plan to entertain informally can use bright party colors.

• Remember that a larger area of the same color is more intense and darker than a small sample indicates. Four orange walls may be too much, while one orange accent wall with three white ones toning it down may be just right.

• If you are unsure of a color's intensity, invest in enough of a sample to cover at least a 6-foot square area. You are better off wasting money on a small amount of a color you do not find appropriate than a larger amount later.

• Always open up any fabric or ask to see sizable samples of such things as wallpaper, upholstery, or carpeting, to get the best possible idea of how it looks in larger quantities.

• Consider tailoring your color scheme to a favorite object. Upholstery fabric, rugs, carpets, paintings, or posters are possible inspirations. If you love the look of an item not intended for the family room, use it as a take-off point anyway.

• Look at the color schemes in magazines and in model rooms, as well as those of your friends.

• Check samples under the same lighting conditions as you will have in your family room. Test colors under fluorescent light, daylight, and filament light.

• Make sure that your family room color scheme does not clash with the color scheme of any adjoining area that is standing open.

Exciting Patterns and Textures

Patterns and textures can bring to life an ordinary color scheme. Some patterns are so captivating that they have been used through the centuries, and textures please the tactile senses as well as the eye. Both are among the most interesting decorating tools.

Modulate your use of textures and patterns as effectively as you do your color scheme. To that end, here are some of the properties to keep in mind.

Patterns

Add zest and zing to the total room scheme by choosing dynamic patterns. To represent a specific period, choose patterns that evoke the colorful days of a favorite time past. Or, be adventurous and use fresh, surprising patterns along with traditional styles.

There are no restrictions on the kinds of patterns you can use in a family room. There are casual and easy-care renditions of almost every traditional kind of pattern or print. One is bound to catch your eye. Exuberant florals, colorful plaids, stripes, checks, abstract prints, representative scenics, geometrics, and tapestry looks are all at your disposal.

In deciding where and what kinds of patterns to use, consider these points.

Pattern can be incorporated anywhere. Floors, walls, and ceilings are candidates. A patterned floor running throughout an especially broken-up area will tend to unify it. It also will make less furniture seem like more in the same space. Patterned walls usually make a room seem smaller. If you want to negate that effect, consider using pattern only on one wall, and coordinate the other three in paint. A patterned ceiling will appear lower than one that is left plain.

Use patterns in relatively broad strokes. How much more effective it is to extend the pattern of your curtains onto the adjoining walls! Consider sweeps of a pattern to avoid broken-up, clustered patterns. Another example would be to cover both a sofa and side chair in the same pattern, or at least make a matching patterned pillow for the chair to extend the pattern of the sofa. Today's patterns often come in coordinated wall coverings and fabric for mix-matching in upholstery, curtains, and wall covering.

Choose a pattern sized according to its use. Some patterns have no definite repeat in the design, but most do. Make sure that the rhythm of the pattern can be seen, by scaling the pattern to its use. For instance, you will want an entire motif to fit onto both the back and seat cushions of an upholstered chair. Or, pick a pattern with sufficient repetition to prevent your wall covering from looking like a disorganized jumble.

Use small patterns to enlarge and large patterns to diminish. Imagine a chair with one huge flower on the back cushion, and one on the seat. Then, picture the same chair with a pattern of small sprays of flowers all over it. The chair will look smaller with the larger pattern. The same principle applies to other areas as well. A large patterned rug or wall covering makes a room look smaller, while a medium-sized pattern extends your sense of perspective, making the room seem larger.

Patterns make things seem closer. If your family room space has long side walls and short, far-away end walls, you can bring the room into better visual proportion by putting a colorful pattern on the end walls. Make the side walls a muted solid tone, and they will recede.

Use directional patterns for height or length. Many patterns have a dominant direction. The most obvious one is the good old stripe. To make rooms seem taller, use the dominant direction vertically. To make a room (or even just a short end wall) seem wider, use the dominant direction horizontally.

Break the rules to create your own effects. Family rooms are for fun, so do not feel locked into any of the above suggestions. For instance, you may opt for a supergraphic in a small family room to give impact, rather than the more traditional small pattern.

Textures

Many of the rules for texture are the same as those for pattern, because textures are often subtle patterns themselves. However, textures have distinctive properties and connotations all their own.

Sleek, shiny, soft, luxurious, rustic, natural, organic, and hard are just some of the textures that can be used together artfully. An interplay of textures gives both tactile and visual interest. Here are some valuable points when choosing textures for a family room.

Choose textures that invite relaxation. Cotton, homespun-looking fabric, shag carpet, suede cloth, leather, and weathered wood are casual textures. They say subtly that this is a room where no one must stand on ceremony.

Use heavy textures in cold rooms. Wool-like upholstery, dark heavily grained woods, and thick carpeting all warm up a large or cold room. The traditional antiqued brick wall, real or manufactured, is another textural touch that embodies warmth and cosiness, through the mental association with brick fireplaces.

Use light, sleek textures in small, hot rooms. See-through glass or shiny plastic, metal surfaces, Formica, Naugahyde, tightly woven fabrics, and metallics or wet-look textures all dispel the sense of confinement and stuffiness in small family rooms. The room will seem cooler, more inviting, and larger.

Glass and chrome make furniture look lighter, so they seemingly take up less room. This furniture comes knock-down and is easy to assemble. A slight separation of levels for the game table area adds architectural interest. (James David furniture)

A Mediterranean feeling is given this room through use of accessories and stained glass windows. Furniture looks like leather and velvet, although it is really made of easy-care fabric. Fireplace stones were whitewashed to add airiness to the room. (James David furniture)

Vary textures in a pleasing array. While you may choose a light or heavy texture for dominant features, spice up the textural balance by drawing on contrasting textures. For instance, contrast a shaggy carpet with a sofa that has a sleek leather look. Or, choose heavily textured paneling for warmth in a room covered with easy-care, shiny resilient flooring. Combine different textures in floor pillows or sofa pillows, and consider carefully the texture of other small accessories, such as lamp shades and bases.

Take samples with you in choosing textures. The easiest way to be sure that textures will work together is to compare them side by side. A satin pillow could be an exciting contrast to a homespun-looking sofa upholstery, or it might make the natural slubbing and thread variations of the linen look rough and unfinished. Generally, the casual fabrics work best with others of the same kind. Be on the lookout for interesting variations and new combinations, to give your textural balance an original look. Feel textures as well as looking at them, and work out combinations that are exciting and pleasant both to see and to touch.

Choosing Family Room Furniture Styles

Furniture styles for family rooms cover the entire gambit of modern designs or historical period styles.

Modular units allow for infinite rearranging into separate units, or can be clustered together as a single conversation pit, as shown. Accessories are kept bare to show off the dominant seating units. Buy as many pieces as you need. (Thayer Coggin furniture)

Almost any traditional style can be found in a rugged rendition with spill-resistant upholstery, scratch- and stain-resistant finishes, and sturdy construction. Many modern materials are naturally impervious to damage, or can be chosen in easy-care materials.

An avid do-it-yourselfer will want to build some of the furniture pieces himself, especially such simple items as bunk bed/couches or perhaps bookcases. Suggestions for designs along these lines are included later in this book.

Others will want to incorporate some of the furniture already on hand for the family room. A tight budget might make garage sales and flea markets your best source for furniture for the family room.

No matter what the source...attic, garage sale, antique store, or furniture retailer...you will want to have a cohesive plan for your family room furnishings. No hodge-podge lodge look will be comfortable hour after hour, year after year.

To pull together the furniture style of your family room, review what you have. This will give you a sense of direction.

• What kind of room are you decorating? Start with the room's character, and list the furniture styles that would go best with it. Do you have a traditional fireplace, or an ultra-contemporary free-standing unit? Does the room have a sunporch feeling that indicates trellises, wicker, bamboo, and garden furniture?

• What's the style of your house? Will a totally modern family room seem jarring in your salt-box colonial-inspired domicile? Will a traditional Early American game room seem out of place in your ranch-style home?

• What furniture style dominates the adjoining rooms? If yours are done in Mediterranean, you might consider carrying over that feeling to the new family room area. It would be especially important to have any family room area that is open to the rest of the house furnished in keeping with other areas. But if the family room is visually enclosed, as a basement room with a stairway entrance would be, you can design a complete departure from the furnishings in the rest of the house.

• What furniture styles do you like best? Which ones do you own now? Your own past pleasure are good guides to the most satisfying choice for a future family room. If you really love a style, do not hesitate to adapt it.

• What furnishings already in hand might be adapted for family room use? This question is a tricky one, because the best advice is to avoid the furniture pieces that you think might "make do." A fresh coat of paint, new upholstery, shortening the legs of an awkward table, putting a new top on a desk-storage center, are all ways of giving an exciting lift to a serviceable furniture piece that would work perfectly well in your family room. But, avoid

An English Tudor feeling comes through in this room through use of leaded glass widows, dark and ornate furniture, brick-like flooring underfoot and behind an interesting bar recess area. The brick is actually an Anso nylon carpet in natural brick colorations. (Allied Chemical Corp.)

Create your own western outpost for your family room with cactus plants and an artistic wall mural. The mural comes by the yard in wall covering by Imperial. (Wallcovering Industry Bureau)

like the plague saddling the new room with a white elephant piece that has not worked out somewhere else in the house. Chances are that it has not worked out elsewhere because you don't really like it, and you won't like it in the recreation or family room, either!

Eclectic Decorating

This term refers to use of widely varied types of furnishings in a cohesive manner. The concept has received much attention in recent years, but it is actually centuries old. The classic Early American Georgian restorations, for example, combine Early American furnishings with a treasure-trove of objects from many lands, brought to these shores in the early trading years. Imari plates from the Orient, Dutch tiles, English silver, French clocks, and Oriental rugs blended together eclectically in those days, and with smashing results.

Then as now, it is the careful attention to how things work well together that makes the difference between successful eclectic decorating and disorder. And, whether you want to try it because you like the freedom and variety it affords, or because you have a group of furnishings that are varied to begin with, it's wise to follow some of the guidelines to successful mix-matching.

Try a color scheme to pull together an eclectic grouping of furnishings. The most unifying schemes are the monochromatic schemes, or those based on neutrals. You can also use woods and wood-looks that are roughly similar. For instance, you might combine butcher block with rattan, bamboo, and popular

golden oak, which are all warm, yellowy and light-colored. In this case, you would pass by pieces that are in darker wood, such as mahogany. Furniture that has relatively undistinguished wood can be painted to match. An example would be a Parsons table surrounded by Victorian country pressed wood chairs, all painted in the same color.

Pattern is another unifying force. Chairs and a couch that formerly looked like distant cousins can become a unit when covered with the same plaid or print. You might go all out and make matching curtains as well.

Oriental artifacts and a bamboo tree in the corner set the tone for this family room. Furniture is kept monotone so that the carpeting becomes the only pattern focus in the room. (Armstrong "Notion" Carpeting)

Keeping large pieces the same style is probably the easiest and most effective way of eclectic decorating. They are the main statements in a room, and once they tell the same style story, the smaller objects can act as secondary voices. This method works well with mostly modern styles, warmed up with accents of old or antique pieces. It also works with mainly traditional, updated with accents of good clean contemporary accessories.

Consider your built-ins as furniture, and finish them according to the free-standing units you plan to use. Treating built-ins as non-furniture, and not relating them to the elements in the room, is one of the commonest furnishing errors committed in family room (or any room) planning.

This light-scale contemporary sofa flips flat to become a queen-size bed with lush, soft cushion. If conventional sleep-sofas do not fit into your decorating scheme, look for inventive units. (Landes furniture)

It takes only a bit more thought and effort to give built-ins such as bars, bookcases, or bunk/couches a furniture-style look. Some examples are included in the last chapter, under '''Easy Built-ins.''

It is still extremely important to have a good idea of styles available when decorating eclectically, since you will choose from every conceivable design source. The following summaries act as guides for setting either the entire scheme of the family room, or as departure points for your own highly personal eclectic combinations.

Early American. A catchall phrase that covers both the styles that were developed here, and those that were brought to these shores from our earliest forefathers. The Pilgrims and pioneers had no time for frills, and native craftsmen were set to the task of making utilitarian pieces that could withstand the rigors of an emerging nation. While some Early American styles are delicate and quite elegant, it is the more countrified, rustic pieces that are most often chosen for family rooms.

Local woods were often used for these pieces, with honest hand-rubbed finishes. Examples are walnut, oak, pine, cherry, and maple. Other furnishings were

(Above) This reproduction is from a trunk originally made in Albany, N.Y. Use versatile and interesting pieces like this one to store extra items that you will not need frequently. Since it is 22" high, it can double as an end table.

Early American furniture (in center photo) is coordinated with period lamps and other accessories, and set on sumptuous rug; room design by Shirley Regendahl.

Cocktail tables (bottom photo) can hold storage, and add nostalgia at the same time. This one is an adaptation of a printer's table, and has drawers on both sides. (Sugar Hill "Front Porch" collection)

A yeoman's chest has a lid that lifts up for storage of bottles or whatever. It is a practical storage unit for any Early American room, and can be placed almost anywhere. (Peters-Revington furniture)

exuberantly painted and hand decorated or stenciled. Examples of the latter are found in Pennsylvania Dutch designs, Hitchcock chairs, or Boston rockers.

Best-loved reproductions of Early American pieces that suit family rooms include tavern tables and chairs, captain's chairs, Windsor chairs, deacon's benches, settles, wagon seats, simple ladder-back and rustic slat-back chairs, wing chairs, candle tables, corner cupboards, blanket and sailor's chests, jelly cupboards, and all manner of countrified tables.

Showcase accessories are often beautiful utilitarian items of times past, such as yarn winders, wagon wheels, and spinning wheels. Smaller accessories include all manner of oil lamps, candle holders, bed warmers, and early fireplace (including cooking) utensils.

Traditional fabrics to use with Early American styles include the homespun looks, patchwork-inspired prints, calicos, checks, plaids, exuberant florals, and American-inspired scenic patterns. Colors were as bright and cheerful as our hard-pressed ances-

tors could make them, with lots of golden yellows, brick-reds, and navy or cobalt-like blues.

Almost any Early American style seems to work well with another Early American style, since the countrified looks all stem from utilitarian sources. And their sense of heritage and natural-textured warmth is highly prized.

Shaker furniture. An Early American style set off by itself. The flowering of Shaker furniture design was in the mid 1800's, although the Shakers arrived in America almost precisely at the time of the Revolution. Religious conviction kept these designers from adding flourishes to their furnishings, giving Shaker-styled furniture an economy of design that is often likened to the best of Modern in purity. A chair rail, high on the wall with pegs to accommodate chairs, and the Shaker ladder-back chair with basket-weave heavy-tape seat and extra-high back, are two Shaker pieces often seen.

Mediterranean styles. Those enjoying recent popularity are massive, in the main. They are derived from 17th century styles that captured the romantic Baroque flavor from Italy, and the Gothic feeling in Spain. Elaborate carving, turning, and massiveness make these pieces suitable for large spaces, and often overbearing in small quarters. Squared lines, geometric carvings on stretchers and legs, and upholstered backs and seats give Mediterranean chairs their drama. Carved fronts and use of elegant dark woods, such as decorative panels of burlwood, give the casement pieces their impressiveness.

Large size end tables, consoles, and coffee tables are favorite pieces, along with Italian chests, credenzas, and tables. Accessory pieces echo the brass nailheads used on the upholstered furniture pieces, or are in geometric wrought-iron designs. Sconces for hefty candles, and massive wood and iron chandeliers (sometimes with colored glass incorporated into the design) are natural accessories.

Fabrics used with Mediterranean furniture should be strong and full of character. Leather and leather looks, combined with the brass studs used on upholstered pieces, are traditional and rich. Velvets, corduroys, and heavy woven fabrics are also good choices. Printed fabrics with a tapestry effect are often chosen. Rich colors are good matchmates for the furniture, including those in jewel tones such as ruby and topaz, or warm gold and orange, or turquoise and emerald.

Mission furniture is a strictly American rendition of Mediterranean styling that originated in the late 1800's and was inspired by the furniture from the Spanish missions in California. Utility of line, squared-off shapes, and functional, relatively plain forms characterize Mission furniture. Slat sides on desks and bookcases often were joined together at the top to make a Gothic-type arch, if not left as just vertical lines. Origi-

This nostalgic piece is a reproduction of a Victorian clam shell banker's desk. Sides roll closed when it is not in use, and it is attractive either open or closed. (Sugar Hill "Front Porch" furniture)

nal pieces are still to be found modestly priced at auctions and antique stores.

Victorian. This style plus other more "nostalgic" furniture styles have gained enormous popularity for family/recreation rooms in recent years. Included in this grouping are the wonderful pieces in golden oak, embellished with elaborate machine-made decorations. The 19th century marked the introduction of machine-made furniture of all sorts, including the development of upholstered seating in which no structural wood parts were exposed.

Tiffany shades, wrought iron floor lamps, and the whole range of fanciful Victorian objects, are ideal accessories for turn of the century furnishings. They are often enhanced by mix-matching with streamlined contemporary furnishings that do not detract from their highly individual lines. Conversely, the Art Nouveau pieces, with shapes taken from the flowing lines of Nature, often work well with other furnishings of a slightly earlier time.

Modern and contemporary furniture. A development of this century, it can be recognized by its freedom from traditional wood supports. Metal, glass, and plastic are all used for frames, and even entire pieces, of furniture. The introduction of these new materials freed the shapes of furniture from the structural basics of the past. New methods of working with both man-made materials and wood have given us a recent heritage of classics that belong to the modern style.

Bentwood furniture developed before the beginning of the 1900's, but is a good early example of

modern thinking. The form of the furniture follows its function, illustrating the beauty of structural, functional use of materials in such a way that function becomes an intrinsic part of the design. When woods are used, the inherent beauty of the grains and texture of the wood, and its malleability in the hands of a craftsman, are used to stunning effect.

Since modern furnishings are often highly functional, they mix well with many other periods when used judiciously. Use them to keep a traditional room from looking like a mini-museum. Besides that, many pieces solve the specific decorating problems of today. Lightweight plastic folding chairs and tables, modular seating and wall storage systems, convertible sofas, glass and steel tables, track lighting fixtures, and easy-care resilient and soft floor covering are all modern additions for convenience as well as style.

Understated modern furniture often benefits with the softening touch of accessories that echo the past in design. Truly revolutionary modern designs are best accessorized with lamps, paintings, and fabrics that are equally in step with our space-age consciousness. Dramatic lighting, modern geometric prints used on upholstery, flooring, and even pop or modernistic wall coverings in rich, exuberant colors, are in keeping with futuristic furnishings.

Since modern furniture does not give us the psychological comfort and nostalgic security of the past, it is wisest to use color combinations that will somewhat soften its impact. For instance, use warm colors to counter the harshness of almost-abstract furnishings. Or, rely on the almost organic, natural colors of a neutral scheme to soften hard modern edges. Plants and flowers operate as natural softeners in modern furnishing schemes.

Swivel chairs are great companions for a fireplace, especially when they also rock. The chair on the left is a rocker-recliner. Both illustrate the kind of lounging-chair comfort you can find for relaxing in a family room. (Comfort-Mates by Pontiac Furniture Industries)

Versatile modules of one, two and three-seat pieces, combined with corner sections, let you arrange this furniture in any shape you want. Large sections are used to avoid any look of legginess. Units are attached by a simple hook arrangement. (Landes furniture)

Problem-Solving Furniture Pieces

In addition to choosing the furniture style that you'd most like to have in your family room, consider what it will add to your convenience and pleasure. There's probably a piece of furniture that will solve whatever decorating problem you have, or that would enrich your enjoyment of your planned room immensely. Here are just some of the pieces from which to choose.

Versatile Seating Units

Modular units are recent additions to furniture styles that function as conversation pits, and can be moved around with a bit of effort for an on-going, ever-changing series of seating arrangements. Often, these are of covered foam, and are big, squishy, and luxurious. Adults who like to sprawl as well as sit will love them. But, if you have small children, make sure that the ample scale of these furniture pieces does not make them uncomfortable.

Equally versatile are the fold-up, stackable, lightweight seating units made of man-made materials. You can remove them to a storage area when not in use. And take a new look at the old-fashioned card table of the past; it and its matching chairs are so stylish you might be tempted to leave them in view for all time. On the other hand, a folding table and chairs are good choices if your entertaining includes cardplaying, but you want to have the furniture stored between parties.

Seating/sleeping combination furniture. These pieces can double as adult guest or slumber party accommodations, and so are good choices for a family/ recreation room. The styles and sizes available today are so numerous, and so unlike their clunky counterparts of a few years back, that it is almost impossible to tell just by looking that a full-sized bed actually is hidden within. They can be found at modest as well as expensive prices, so you can use their added versatility without destroying your budget.

Most units work best for one function, with sacrifices in performance in the other. The most comfortable units for sleeping may have a bulkier look than you might have wanted, while the units that look best for seating may not have the mattress support you would want in a full-time bed. Decide which function is most important to you and work out a compromise. If you will have overnight guests using the unit frequently, make sure that the mattress is healthful and comfortable. No one likes to visit and suffer through a bad night's sleep on lumpy, second-rate bedding.

In choosing a convertible furniture piece, be sure it is easy to open and close. Test the mechanism more than once, and take into consideration the amount of room the unit requires when opened for sleeping. You will want to actually lie down on the mattress part to test it, just as you would a regular bed. Then, test it for comfort while sitting as well.

Your convertible might be as simple as a built-in bunk/couch. Just be sure that you plan the piece with sufficient space for comfortable sleeping, side to side and lengthwise.

Invisible Storage

Storage units are a necessity if you have hobbies. You may want to use family room storage units to accommodate items from window fans to formal gowns, if space is at a premium throughout your house. Handsome storage solutions include end-table units that are actually little chests or cubes that open. Other examples are captain's bunks that have storage drawers underneath. You even can find coffee tables that have enclosed sections for records and games, or anything else you want to have right at hand. Antique trunks look great with a little refinishing in paint or paper, or reduced to their original wood. Use them as storage end tables, or coffee tables, depending upon height.

To determine your storage needs, start by dividing things into those that you'll want within easy reach, and those you use infrequently. A coffee-table trunk, opened from the top, is no place to store things you use every few days, since you will have to move everything to get to what is inside. It might be ideal, however, for storage of Christmas ornaments or patio table accessories during the winter, or a collection of slides.

Storage units with fixed shelves are less versatile than those with adjustable ones. However, if you have specific items to store, it might be most convenient in the long run to have the interior of a storage unit specifically set up to accommodate these pieces. A good example would be a unit designed to hold tape cassettes or records.

Remember, also, to consider future acquisitions in the storage requirements for your family room. Otherwise, within a year or so, you will outgrow all the work you put into the new room.

Modular Wall Units

Relatively recent design developments, these units work both as a decorative focus and for storage. These are highly recommended if you are not sure you will be staying in the current house, because you can take them along should you decide to move. They also are good choices if your handyman skills are not sufficient to build your own wall units. Another time to consider modular wall units is when built-ins might be out of keeping with the furniture style you have chosen, unless finished with great care and the use of precious woods. In this case, modulars might cost you less in the long run.

Other modules of this wall system can be adapted for use other than entertaining, but this one works well as a discreet bar. Formica finishes include butcher block, pecan, white, yellow, and brown. (Interlock Furniture)

You can find a modular wall system that is in almost any conceivable style, and to store almost any kind of object. By definition, they are wall units combined of components that make up the best combination for you. In most cases, you can choose from modules that are designed for open book storage, enclosed cabinets, hi-fi or television storage, foldout desks, foldout bars, and drawer units. You are totally free to make up the combination that best suits your wall space and needs.

Modular wall units give an impressive sweep to any wall where they are used. Consider them as much of a design statement in the room as any other major wall treatment or furniture piece.

Your best choice would be to buy all the units within a modular system right at the beginning. If finances simply won't allow this, check with the store or manufacturer to see if they give any guarantees as to the length of time they will continue producing the specific line that you have purchased. Try to make sure that you will be able to complete your system. Some systems are such classics that they will probably be produced for many years to come.

Refreshment Centers

There are many good reasons for setting up a permanent eating/refreshment center in a family room. As an alternate eating area, it is ideal for teenagers, who like to entertain their own friends without interfering with the kitchen activities. If your cookouts take place close to the family room, especially if they are on another floor of the house, having a miniature kitchen nearby will save time and steps. And, children will feel less restrained in a family room snack area, which has been designed spill-proof. Finally, you might want to use it for your own entertaining.

Even if the family/recreation room is right off the kitchen, it would be a great convenience to have a separate area where drinks can be mixed. That way, you avoid a traffic jam at the kitchen sink during the cocktail hour. Or you can add a full wet bar for entertainment purposes.

One of the first considerations in setting up a refreshment center is whether it will be convenient to add a necessary water supply. Even without a water source, you can set up a mini-food serving area; it can be a permanent installation, such as a bar, or a portable unit that can be opened for use and then disguised to blend into the surroundings. Your own entertaining pattern will determine the best solution for your family room.

Another point is that the seating and serving area must be convenient for all who will use it. This means

If you really do not want a bar look in your family room at all times, try a unit like this. Stools are stored inside the bar when not used, and the top flips up to become a solid lid. The home refreshment center is on casters. (Chromcraft furniture)

child-comfortable chairs instead of stools, if need be. And, if meals will be one mainstay here, then the narrow kind of drinking bar favored by adults during parties, will be less suited to your needs.

Once a comfortable drinking and eating area has been established, your other factors are the food and drink preparation units themselves. Today, there are a host of miniaturized cooking appliances that easily can be put into play in a game room. Assuming that you will do your main cooking in the kitchen, your needs here may only be for short-order or re-warming cooking that could well be handled by small electrical appliances.

A small refrigerator in the family room is both practical and convenient. Use it to stock snack beverages on a day-to-day basis, and use it as an additional cold storage area for parties. Ice will be at hand whenever

you need it, without many trips to the kitchen refrigerator. You will have less wear and tear on your full-size kitchen unit, and avoid the constant opening and closing of it, by keeping snacks in the family room unit.

One cautionary note: you may want to table putting any electrical or cooking units into a family room used primarily as a playroom for very small children. Safety suggests that such appliances should not be left in the same space unattended, until unsupervised children are old enough to know how to use them or to stay away from them.

Storage

To make your refreshment center as convenient as possible, plan a storage area for glassware, dishes, utensils and flatware. Whether your entertaining calls for elegant, cut crystal highball glasses, or casual paper plates and plastic, you will want them within easy reach.

Plan the family room eating/drinking area as carefully as you would any dining area. Make sure that the lighting is flattering and attractive (see later discussion under "Ceilings") and that the surroundings are interesting. For instance, if your best plan is to place a bar along the wall with chairs or stools in front of it, pay particular attention to the wall behind the bar. A mirror, a mural, shelves filled with interesting objects, paintings, or other zestful decoration will set a festive mood.

A compact, less complicated refreshment center would be the best solution if elaborate food serving is not in your plans. Or you can, of course, try to bring everything you need in from the kitchen, a less expensive

This home entertainment unit is specifically designed to store and display family room favorites. Allow space to display objects, such as baskets or vases, and to make wall storage systems interesting and artistic. ("System VI" from Interlock Furniture)

This coffee table folds into a cube when dancing floor space is needed. The sides fold down, so closed, it can be used for party storage. The cypress wood is emphasized with picture-window framed side panels. (Trend line furniture)

and less convenient system. Specialized furniture pieces are available that cater exactly to this need. Some are movable food caddies, complete with an alcohol-proof surface for drink preparation, and storage for potables and glasses within. Tea wagons are classic examples of this sort of unit, and come in a wide array of styles. A modern one has a butcher-block surface and bicycle wheels; others resemble consoles that match other furniture pieces in the styles often chosen for family rooms. In a small-size family room, a unit that can be shifted out of the way when not in use may be the best solution to the space squeeze.

Another compact solution is units that are stationary, but take up little space. Carefree surfaces and well-designed storage for ice buckets, glasses, and beverages are usual features of these units.

Furniture Material

Easy care upholstered furniture has become so much a part of furnishing offerings that almost any style is available in a no-fuss, resistant fabric. Synthetics are constantly being improved, and offer good stain resistance and cleaning ease. There are also other fabrics treated for stain resistance and long wear.

Always check into the exact qualities guaranteed or claimed by the manufacturer in the upholstery you choose. It goes without saying that you will not want this room to be burdened with fragile, fussy, formal fabrics that inhibit true relaxation.

The beloved leather looks that abound in casual furniture styles are also wonderful for family rooms. In choosing them make sure that they are as comfortable as they look, without a "plastic" coldness to the touch. Good imitation leathers these days are almost as luxurious as the real thing, but light-years ahead in easy care. Most need just the wipe of a damp cloth.

Be equally persistent in seeking out easy-care upholstery for any pieces you might make yourself. If a fabric you have chosen is not stain-resistant, investigate the stain-proofing materials that you can buy and do it yourself, or ask your cleaner if he can have it professionally done for you. From slipcover to throw pillow, your family room will be more fun if you need not have to worry about constant cleaning.

One added way to cut down on cleaning is to choose upholstery fabrics that show soil the least. Either extreme in the lightness and darkness spectrum will show soil more than the same color in a medium tone. Imagine salt on a black vinyl sofa, or soot on a white leather-look chair, and you will see how such color extremes demand more attention.

Any patterned upholstery is more soil-disguising than a solid fabric. Good coverups include prints, plaids, and tweeds, or antiqued leather looks. Do not feel that you must totally avoid the solids, or deeply dark or starkly light colors. But if your family is more inclined to put feet up on the furniture than to plant them firmly on the floor, then limit easily soiled fabrics to smaller pieces, such as accessory chairs or pillows.

Hard Surfaces

Carefree hard surfaces are even easier to find than easy-care upholstery, and doubly convenient in a family room. Plastic finishes come in woodgrains that closely simulate the real thing. Natural woods are often protected with finishes that are impervious to spotting or staining, even with alcohol. Plastic and metal are naturally sturdy, as are tile surfaces.

Manufacturers of such necessary furniture pieces as tables and frames of casual furniture often specify exactly what the surfaces are resistant to, and include guarantees for performance. Reading the fine print can save you much future aggravation and anguish.

Choosing a Theme

If your family/recreation room is primarily intended for family parties, consider building party-type decorations right into the decor. Use a festive theme to tie your decoration all together.

Just how far you will want to carry the theme in decorating your family room depends upon your needs for versatility within the room, and your own desire for a change of pace. For instance, a South Seas background, which might be great fun for parties, would be a bit unnerving if you also use the room for Sunday painting. And a theme as specific as this would become tiresome much sooner than a more general background decor.

The theme you choose for a family room will work best if it is an extension of real family interests. For instance, if home movies are favorites of you all, and the room is set up for projection, then you might choose a Hollywood theme. Another possibility is to decorate in a fanciful way totally unrelated to your own general lifestyle, for a complete change of pace; a New Orleans Mardi Gras theme is an example.

Sample Themes

By adding easy-to-change touches that bring a theme to life, you can easily alter it to suit later tastes. The trend today is toward multi-purpose rooms that are not locked into one prevailing theme. However, most rooms can be adapted to a theme look just with the addition of a few clever accessories, pictures, or do-it-yourself additions in paint or plywood.

Here is a smattering of theme ideas, with some suggestions on how to begin with them.

Furniture echoes European car seats and wallpaper identifies this family's interest in car rallies. (Imperial Wallcovering, Collins & Aikman carpeting)

The paneling, brick hearth and mantle, country furniture, and Franklin stove all create this family room's theme. (Western Wood Products Assn.)

Country motifs. These include stables, barns, chalets, and western decorations. Weathered wood such as barn siding used inside helps simulate these effects. Seating and storage areas can be made to look like stalls, with half-door effects on the walls. Wagon wheels, old lanterns, bridles, water buckets, yokes, and animal prints are good accessories. Cobblestone or brick resilient flooring fits right in.

For a western theme, horseshoes, branding irons, and even cactus plants add to the effect. Bars can be built to simulate frontier town saloons, and western music fans can display guitars.

Taverns, inns, and pubs. Favorite motifs include Early American inns and taverns, elegant wine cellar effects, simulated English pubs, and French bistros. Each has its own distinctive accessories.

Early American inns often include settles around an inviting fireplace, tavern tables and simple chairs, candle sconces, braided rugs, and wide-plank flooring. Warm wood paneling heightens the illusion. For avid card players, such a theme lends itself to a handsome arrangement of tables set up for cardplaying at a moment's notice. Pewter accessories and homespun upholstery, plus tavern signs for a bar area, can lend authenticity.

Wine cellars are simulated with the simple technique of creating a wine bottle wall. Do it by stacking innumerable small wine racks, or make a huge wine rack that covers one entire wall. Used bottles as well as filled ones are handy and flavorful decorations. Wine labels and wine crate ends can cover a decorative bar area. Soft lighting and a sense of elegant enclosure will make this room a favorite for after-dinner entertaining.

English pubs are often simulated with the use of paneling and frosted glass or mirrors. Brass and copper accessories and the traditional dart board help the illusion, as will any traditional British object, such as the Union Jack.

French bistros and sidewalk cafés are translated through the use of small marble-topped tables and circular awning umbrellas. Almost any Toulouse Lautrec poster will definitely establish this theme, and act as a source for the color scheme as well.

Mediterranean motifs. These include Italian Grottos, Mexican/Spanish motifs, and some of our Southwestern Indian inspirations. One thing common to them all is the use of stucco on the walls, and white or light pastel colors. This theme could be particularly stunning to counteract a room that is naturally dark.

Grottos can include niches in the walls for the displaying of favorite objects. Bright colors that reflect off of the stucco walls and the use of Italian flags would also contribute. Mexican/Spanish motifs are bright and cheery. Wrought iron can be used for sconces and accents, as can the massive furniture common to both cultures. Bright reds, oranges, and pinks in shawls, fans, rugs, paper maché, and flowers give a room a south-of-the-border look.

American Indian inspired rooms can be the most sumptuous and sophisticated ones around. Pottery, baskets, blankets, plenty of simulated suede, and soft earth-tones as a background for stone or wood or clay artifacts will create a natural, earthy but elegant motif.

Exotic lands. The simple addition of ethnic fabrics and a few accessories from a faraway land can totally theme a party room. Favorite inspiring countries and their effects are:

Japan. Use sliding screens, low tables, silk pillows on the floor and on platforms covered with straw matting, and a pebbled garden area with artistic planting. An ideal atmosphere for resting, reading, music enjoyment or contemplation.

South Seas. Use beautiful batik upholstery, lattice work in wicker or rattan, plenty of plants in straw-covered pots.

African. Use the wonderful African artifacts and carvings plus the exciting and exuberant fabrics that come from that part of the world.

India. Draped fabrics of madras can cover the walls and seating areas. Mysterious brass accessories and hanging lamps will complete the illusion, as will ornate Indian upholstered animals used as accessories.

Favorite sports. You need not be a semi-pro to design your room around a favorite sport. Even if the beginners' slope is as far as you are likely to get, you may want to turn your family room into a miniature ski lodge. By using a family sport for the main theme of the family room, cumbersome equipment can be integrated into the room's design. For instance, crossed skis on the walls add to the atmosphere, and dispose of one storage problem. Other sports to theme a family room include football, bowling, tennis, flying, surfing, sailing and boating, or a general nautical look.

The arts and entertainment. Wonderful graphics abound from movies and the theater. Playbills, posters and pictures of stars, give instant excitement to a family room. Art Deco accessories that look as though they came from the lobbies of the most world-famous theaters will complete the picture.

Children's playroom themes. Choose children's themes that are slightly more sophisticated than the age level of your children, so that they will last as your children grow. For instance, nursery story characters are quickly outgrown, while cowboys and Indians are likely to last for some years.

Supergraphic numbers and letters in bright colors are cheerful decorations for children's playrooms and stand the test of time. Other fanciful themes include circus decoration or zoo and other wild animal motifs. One method is to use bright colors in furniture and set aside a poster-wall (or roll-down sheet of drawing paper on a wall) where current interests of the children can be displayed and changed as necessary.

Whether you choose from some of these suggested themes or decide on one that is entirely different, make sure that it is a theme that truly reflects your own interests and needs. You are better off keeping the decor general and inviting than in choosing a theme that really does not fit you. After all, themes are just ways of giving the room added personality. And the main personality of the room, regardless of how it is decorated, is you and your interests.

Earth-toned colors and natural textures of Mexican tile and Navajo blankets give this room its Southwest atmosphere. (Majestic Fireplaces)

Matched sofas are placed in an "L" arrangement, affording a good view of the fireplace from both. The traffic pattern goes before the coffee table, so it would be easy to serve refreshments without interfering with conversation in this room. (Stratford sofas and Peters-Revington tables)

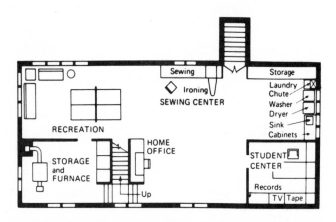

A separate student center was created in this plan to reduce possible stereo noise irritation. Note that sewing and laundry centers are close and convenient to one another, and separated from the relaxation corner of the room. (Floorplans from Bilco Company)

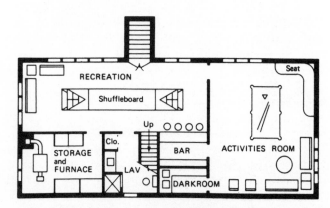

More activities created a need for more divisions in this basement recreation room arrangement. Teen and adult hosts can entertain separately, but at the same time. (Floorplans from Bilco Company)

grouping. If you arrange half of a conversational grouping on one side of a traffic lane and the other beyond it, you will find that people cut right through the seating grouping. An alternative would be to arrange a seating grouping with perhaps a side chair blocking that walkway, while providing a clear walkspace behind the seating grouping. Make sure that your seating is near integral room features or items, such as a fireplace or television set.

Sketch in your main traffic lanes on your room layout, showing paths from doorways. Then you can sketch in the secondary traffic lanes, to make sure that going from one area to another of your furniture arrangement is equally convenient.

Allow Workable Space for Furnishings

Try to follow these guidelines in keeping furniture close enough for gracious conversation, yet far enough apart to avoid crowding. Check your arrangements against these criteria:

- Main traffic lanes should be at least 4 feet wide; minor ones 2 feet wide.

- Doorways need 3 feet of free space into the room; outside entrances need 4 feet.

- Drawer storage cabinets call for 40 inches in front.

- Closets need 36 inches of clearance in front.

- Seating space at a worktable or desk takes up 36 inches.

- Dining areas need 32 inches for a person to rise from a chair; 36 inches for someone to squeeze past a seated person.

- Sofas and chairs require a minimum of 18 inches in front of them.

- Remember to plan for the extension of reclining chairs.

- Frequently used bookcases need 18 inches minimum clearance.

Plan Comfortable Closeness

Unless you have a hermit in the house, arrange your furnishings so that no seating remains stranded. For comfortable conversation, the maximum distance between seated persons is 8 feet. If the distance be-

4. Furniture Arrangements

Only you know the activities that will take place in your family room, and the main furniture pieces that you will need. The next step is to work out a good arrangement of the elements included. Furniture arranging goes hand in hand with the planning of wall areas, floor space, and other defining features. By working with the furniture templates included in this chapter, you can decide such issues as which areas could be devoted to a workshop; where the main seating arrangement should be placed; how lighting should be located to spotlight activities; or, where hobby areas could be located.

If you are finishing off an area such as the basement, start by roughing in your furniture arrangement first. While you can always adjust your furniture arrangements to fit into stationary space, it is 100 times easier to create a successful floor plan when wall divisions (or partitions or dividers) are planned to accommodate the furniture that will be placed within them. Then, you can avoid such aggravating problems as the fireplace located so that it is impossible to arrange a comfortable conversational grouping around it, the wall just six inches too short to take the loveseat unit that rightfully belongs there; or, the conversational grouping split in two by the room's main traffic stream.

Convenience and good sense are the two main ingredients of successful furniture arrangements. Looks come last. Once the furniture is conveniently located, you can accessorize it to achieve balance and unity. The steps involve making a layout on paper with the templates provided, working out the comfortable spaces that must be left free around furniture pieces, plotting the traffic patterns that will occur in your room, and coming up with the best placement of the furniture involved.

Using the Templates

The templates shown here from Ethan Allen, Inc., represent the popular furniture pieces found in a home, scaled to ¼ inch equals one foot. You can photocopy these into as many sets as you need to make various arrangements, using the pieces that approximate the furniture you actually have or plan to

have. Or, you can make cutouts of your own furniture shapes and sizes.

Bedding units are included since you may be using your family room for extra sleeping. You also can use the bedding shapes to illustrate for yourself what arrangements are necessary when a sleep sofa is opened.

Start by Carefully Outlining the Existing Room

Measure all the walls and doorways of your family room area, being careful to be exact in scaling them to the ¼-inch graph paper. Use the symbols shown, such as those for doors, radiators, and electrical outlets, in defining the walls. Remember to include such items as pipes or protrusions that cannot be moved, and architectural features such as built-ins, stairway platforms, or fireplaces.

You can use the same floor plan to assist in making layouts for ceiling tiles or floorcoverings. By accurately and carefully making your first layout, you can revise it for later updating jobs.

Make Cutouts of your Furniture Pieces.

If you do not wish to use the pieces included in this book, copy them onto tracing paper to make your own set. One advantage to this latter method is that you can also color them to approximate the colors of the actual furniture pieces you plan to use, to get an idea of your overall color scheme balance. In any case, be sure to identify each cutout with a description of the furniture piece it represents. You may want to back these templates with cardboard, so that they will wear well through shuffling and reshuffling. Record the dimensions of your furniture as a shopping guide. Note seat, back, and arm heights, table heights, as well as top-view dimensions.

Establish Traffic Patterns

You can alter traffic patterns somewhat through the arrangement of furniture, but the closer they are to natural traffic patterns, the more convenient they will be. Natural patterns often are direct lines from doorway to doorway, or from doorway to the main seating

Cut-Out Templates

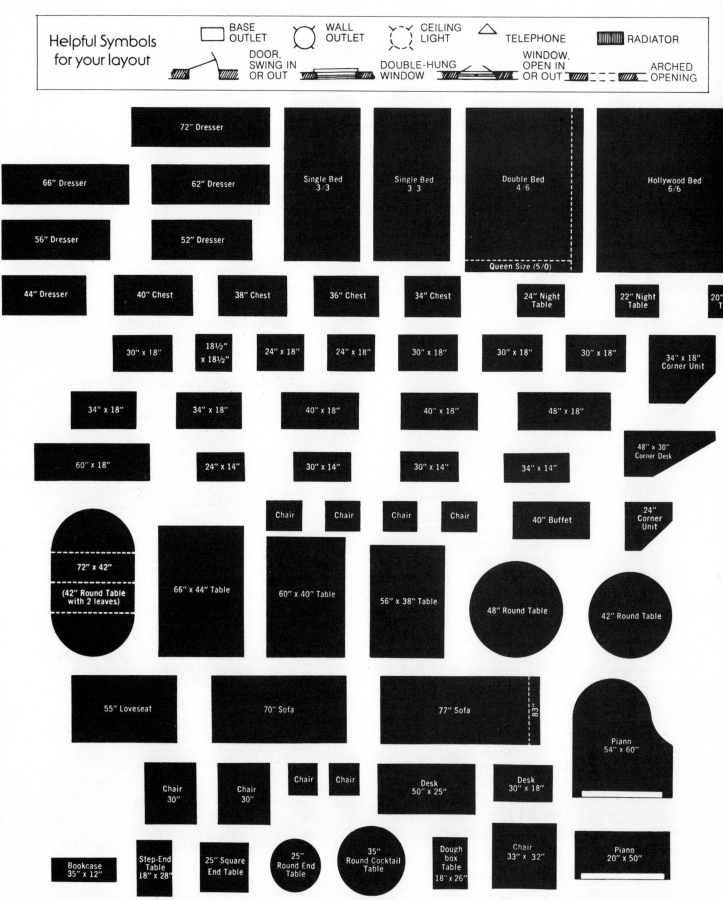

Helpful Symbols for your layout

BASE OUTLET
WALL OUTLET
CEILING LIGHT
TELEPHONE
RADIATOR
DOOR, SWING IN OR OUT
DOUBLE-HUNG WINDOW
WINDOW, OPEN IN OR OUT
ARCHED OPENING

72" Dresser

66" Dresser
62" Dresser

56" Dresser
52" Dresser

Single Bed 3/3
Single Bed 3/3
Double Bed 4/6
Queen Size (5/0)
Hollywood Bed 6/6

44" Dresser
40" Chest
38" Chest
36" Chest
34" Chest
24" Night Table
22" Night Table
20" Table

30" x 18"
18½" x 18½"
24" x 18"
24" x 18"
30" x 18"
30" x 18"
30" x 18"
34" x 18" Corner Unit

34" x 18"
34" x 18"
40" x 18"
40" x 18"
48" x 18"

60" x 18"
24" x 14"
30" x 14"
30" x 14"
34" x 14"
48" x 30" Corner Desk

Chair
Chair
Chair
Chair
40" Buffet
24" Corner Unit

72" x 42" (42" Round Table with 2 leaves)
66" x 44" Table
60" x 40" Table
56" x 38" Table
48" Round Table
42" Round Table

55" Loveseat
70" Sofa
77" Sofa
83"
Piano 54" x 60"

Chair 30"
Chair 30"
Chair
Chair
Desk 50" x 25"
Desk 30" x 18"

Bookcase 35" x 12"
Step-End Table 18" x 28"
25" Square End Table
25" Round End Table
35" Round Cocktail Table
Dough box Table 18" x 26"
Chair 33" x 32"
Piano 20" x 50"

(Templates courtesy of Ethan Allen, Inc.)

comes too large, consider arranging seating groupings into more than one unit. And, arrange secondary seating groupings to include more than one chair. Another rule of thumb is that a conversational grouping of more than eight people becomes difficult. Your parties will be livelier if you divide seating groupings into smaller units; then, everyone has a reasonable chance to interact.

Plan access to your conversational grouping to prevent newcomers having to crawl over those already seated. Some of the newer conversation pits demand such shifting and moving because they are very enclosed, but that is part of their casual style. More conventional seating is best served with secondary paths so that guests can come and go from the group as they please.

For day to day convenience as well as for parties, check that adequate lighting, a surface to hold a book or a snack, and an ashtray space for smokers, is right at hand for every seating space. Coffee tables or end tables can provide surfaces.

If yours is a foots-up family, don't forget hassocks or coffee tables that allow for sprawling. Include them and the space they require in your floor plan.

Creating a Center of Interest

Your room may already have a center of interest ...a natural focus for your room that immediately leads and captivates the eye. It may be a wonderful view from a large picture window; another obvious center of interest is a fireplace. Forcefully accessorize these natural focuses to make them even more dramatic.

If your room does not have a natural focus, then create one. Examples are: a collection of paintings on an accent wall painted a different color; a mural on the key wall; a sizable painting or wall hanging, such as an interesting rug. An attractive bookcase, either built-in or free-standing, is a center of interest when it displays art objects or collections (with proper shelf lighting to show them off). You can even add an artificial fireplace that needs no special venting, or an indoor plant center. In most cases, you will want to arrange your major seating grouping around the center of interest.

Conversational Groupings

Try several conversational groupings around the center of interest in your room plan, to see which works best. One of the basic arrangements, or a variation, should suit the space you have. You might also use one of these arrangements for a secondary grouping in the same room.

You do not have to create your own "U" arrangement when units such as this one come ready-made. Back pillows come off the side sofas, which double as beds. An armless loveseat is used to complete the back of the "U". (Trend Line Furniture)

1. "U" Shapes. The base can be the sofa, flanked on either side with chairs. Generally, you will want to keep the side pieces smaller to allow easy access to the center of this arrangement. The new conversation pits are handsome renditions of the "U" seating arrangement.

2. "L" Shapes. The long side usually is the sofa (or built-in), flanked on one side by an additional sofa, loveseat-sized unit, or matched chairs. Another variation of the "L" shape is the use of two built-in units, hugging the walls of a corner. Additional chairs can be angled to face the "L", creating a conversational circle.

This version of the "L" arrangement can be worked out with solid built-in-looking furniture. These are sectional, with the end table an integral part of each piece. (Milo Baughman design for Thayer Coggin)

This large space needed an open storage wall to serve as a division between seating and the game table area. Note that the couch and matching loveseat are placed in the classic "L" shape, with an extra chair that can be pulled up whenever wanted. (Chromcraft furniture)

3. "ll" Shapes. In this arrangement, seating units are placed directly across from each other, often with an attractive coffee table in the center. A sofa on one side might be augmented with two large chairs opposite it. Or, matching loveseats or sofas can be placed face to face. In small spaces, matched chairs can form the two sides of the "ll" arrangement.

Variations on these themes are endless. In many cases, you'll want to have a basic seating arrangement that is stationary. Supplement it by pulling up occasional seating pieces from other areas of the room for parties. And, if the arrangement seems too static, you can angle chairs for a less formal alignment.

Experiment with the placement of your furniture groupings in relation to all your walls, but especially to

To cope with small space, keep furnishings streamlined and simple, arranged with clean lines. Here is a "ll" arrangement of couch and matched chairs, lined up to give everyone a fireplace view. The wall covering adds needed pattern. (Wallcovering Industry Bureau)

Matched loveseats in a "II" arrangement are an ideal answer to a long and narrow room. Cozy conversations are bound to take place with this intimate arrangement. Attractive wall covering ties the game table area to the rest of the room. (Imperial wall covering, Chromcraft Furniture, Collins & Aikman carpeting)

Placing these two sofas in a "II" allows a view of the fire-place (to the right) from the dining table. The family room is off the kitchen, with the dining table placed between the two areas, convenient for meals and ready to double for cards. (Trend Line furniture)

the center of interest. Your furniture need not be clustered directly before the focus wall to be related to it. What is important is that the focus wall is the logical vista from the main seating grouping, and that the view is relatively unobstructed. For instance, you might flank your masterpiece painting with a secondary seating arrangement on either side, but place the main seating on the opposite wall.

Another arrangement in a large room would be to place a sofa near the room's center, directly across from the focus, with an attractive table behind it and a logical traffic path behind that. You can create a greater feeling of intimacy by bringing furniture into the room, away from the walls. In contrast, if space is a problem, moving your furniture out to the perimeter of the room will make it seem larger.

Diagonal seating arrangements are also exciting, and sometimes the very best means of coping with a difficult traffic pattern or general layout. For instance, a diagonal "U" seating arrangement can be just the ticket for a room with a corner fireplace, since it allows each person a good view of the fire.

For fireplaces, always keep in mind the lines of sight for fire viewing when arranging furniture. Seating that is flush to the wall on either side is totally frustrating to the dedicated fireplace watcher.

In a large room, you may want your conversational grouping away from the fire but within clear view of it. An answer would be to use two chairs in an "ll" arrangement flanking the fireplace, in such a way that they do not impede the view from the main seating area. How even more luxurious if these chairs swivel for cozy fireside sitting, when there are just two of you.

If you are planning to install a fireplace of your own, consider the corner units. Often, by placing a Franklin stove or similar unit at an angle, you increase the possibilities for a workable seating arrangement to take full advantage of it.

Picture windows call for the same adherence to sight lines as do fireplaces. Keep any seating placed in front of the windows light and movable if your main seating is across the room.

Another factor in decorating around a picture window is how it looks at night. Decorative shades will liven up and replace the view that dominates by daytime. Or, if you really love your view, your best decorating tool might be outdoor lighting so that your vista becomes even more magical, and visible, after sundown.

Sliding doors offer the same possibilities as picture windows, but with the added trickiness of their having to provide access. Start by placing your arrangement somewhat away from the doors so that anyone coming in does not seem to burst upon those seated. Then, allow enough room for that person to move gracefully around the seating area instead of having to come right through it. Generally, this is accomplished by shifting the seating so that the focus is on the stationary side of the sliding door rather than the movable one.

If you are installing sliding doors yourself, figure out your arrangement before designating which door is to be stationary and which is to move. Your seating arrangement is also a factor in determining exactly where to locate each door on the wall.

Since nobody wants a view of muddy galoshes, make sure that any door that acts as a design feature for your family/recreation room has the needed storage space that accompanies coming and going. This might include an attractive cabinet outdoors for barbecue equipment that cannot be moved, or a ski and sled center out of the sight in the room. A blanket chest beside the doors on the inside can serve for removing boots and clothing and to store the boots as well.

Integrating Other Elements

Sometimes a stairway, entertainment center, or entrance to the kitchen side of a kitchen/family room is unique and attractive enough that it becomes a welcome contribution to the room. More often than not, it is an area that calls for integration without emphasis. Here are some of the ways these areas are successfully handled.

Stairways

Stairways are visual as well as physical bridges from one area to another, so they must reflect both areas they join. One method is to use a color common to both schemes. Another technique is to use multicolored artwork as stepping stones from the top to the bottom floors.

An open stairway treatment is a good choice if you want the spillover of light from the upper floor to add to the general illumination of the family room. It also makes the room seem larger. Half walls along the length of the staircase partially achieve this effect, while some staircases can be constructed to practically seem to float on the wall to which they are joined.

An enclosed staircase is the best choice if you need ample wall space, or if the angle or other aspects of the staircase act as disruptive design factors in the overall room. These staircases act as entrance halls for the family room, and can be decorated with a character all their own, so long as they retain a kinship to the rooms they join.

Regardless of the kind of staircase you have or plan to add, be sure to provide the four feet of clearance at the top and bottom into the rooms. Safety is a key factor in any basement staircase design, and that includes adequate lighting for the entire length of the staircase. Make sure that there are switches at both the bottom and top of the steps, and that the lights are placed so that people do not walk down the staircase in their own shadow. Add proper railings and safety treads as additional safety factors.

If the staircase entrance into the room is the one most often used, make sure the first, walk-in view of the room is exciting and inviting. Accent walls are often positioned opposite the main entrance for just this reason. Check your furniture arrangements to make sure that the angles created are going to be attractive from the staircase.

Entertainment Centers

Entertainment centers, such as bars, are almost always strong design statements in a room, but often

Basement entryway stairs in an existing (or new) area are easily installed with heavy, 14-gauge steel stringers nailed to the areaway sidewall.

Standard 2x10 lumber treads slide into slots in the stringers and are anchored with nails. The treads may later be removed if necessary (when bringing bulky items into the basement) to leave the whole areaway free and clear.

do not function well as the center of interest. For one thing, the back of the stools or chairs that are conveniently placed on the room side of a snack bar are not exciting for constant viewing. Unless your bar area is truly unique (such as having a major wall decoration in the back), treat the entire area as a secondary seating grouping.

One good way of doing this is to use the space needed behind the stools to create a walking corridor. Another is to visually set off the entire area through the use of contrasting colors.

Kitchen/Family Room Entrances

Kitchen/family rooms call for the same consideration. In most cases, you will want to orient your seating arrangement so that it faces away from the cooking areas. In this way, those seated will not be irritated by looking directly into the lighting you need for cooking. And, meals served in a dining section of a family/kitchen room can be cleaned up without the cook being center stage.

Attractive half-walls that separate the kitchen from the family room area can be paneled or painted to match the furnished area. If your cabinets are on view, you may want to use them as a key to the furnishings of your family room.

In combining a kitchen and family room area it is important that the main entrance to the family room not be directly through the cooking area. This is not only inconvenient, it can be dangerous. A solution is to reorganize the kitchen so that the main functions are not divided by a traffic lane. Although this may call for shifting a doorway, rehanging some cabinetry, or reorganizing appliances, it is the kind of beforehand planning that will pay off in convenience.

Relocating Doorways and Positioning Windows

The merest breezethrough of these pages shows that what goes into the room is a major factor in the successful use of its space. And in some cases, your best bet is to undertake such a major change as moving a doorway, adding a window, or creating a partition. All of these projects are more expensive than merely imposing your furniture needs onto existing space, but might be the necessary solution. Although these are projects that handy persons can take on themselves with the help of books that delve into construction techniques, this is also the point at which many will want to consult a remodeler. You will definitely want professional guidance when it comes to working with load-bearing walls, and perhaps will need a professional's help to make sure that local building codes are complied with.

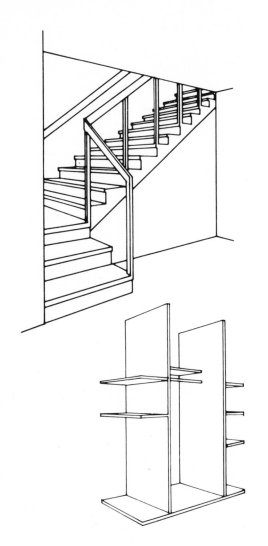

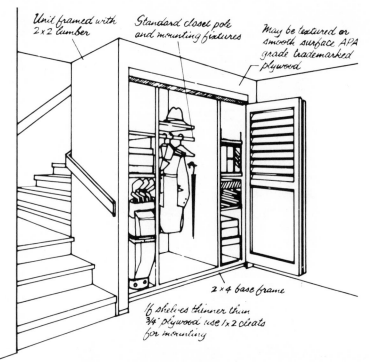

Unit framed with 2 x 2 lumber

Standard closet pole and mounting fixtures

May be textured or smooth surface APA grade trademarked plywood

2 x 4 base frame

If shelves thinner than 3/4" plywood use 1 x 2 cleats for mounting

The stairway space is often wasted by both builder and homeowner. This closet interior is organized for outdoor clothing, golf clubs, etc., and you can match it to walls with paint or wall covering.

Use your furniture templates to make sure that you can't solve your arrangement problems with clever use of the space at hand before you undertake any major revisions. More often than not, you can find a workable solution merely by being creative in your furniture arrangement.

5. Getting the Room Ready

Some of the work that goes into creating a successful family or recreation room may not show at all; still, it should be done at the very beginning. Into this category fall the insulation, supplementary heating and ventilation, additional plumbing for a bath or kitchen, wiring and lighting if built in, and the addition of a fireplace or Franklin stove. It is a good idea to give any staircase leading to the new retreat a once-over as well, since it may need modification.

Repairs

Start by coming to grips with any basic repair problem that might be present, such as water leakage. In many homes, the potential family room space in the basement or elsewhere is sound and dry, needing only the additions listed above and some finishing details. However, make sure your new decor will not be covering up some basic problem that will resurface to plague you, and ruin your finished family room. Since many family rooms are located in basements, here is a handy list of areas to check for potential problems. Finding any or all of these might require the assistance of a contractor in correcting them. The repairs should be made before you go any further.

Walls

Check walls for cracks or leaks. A crack can be repaired inside by removing the crumbled material and filling it with fresh crack filler. There are special fillers

A converted garage makes use of a split level and massive fireplace to give all the architectural interest a room would need. Note that the raised hearth allows good viewing from any seat. (Carpeting by Milliken of Anso nylon, by Allied Chemical Corp.)

Space-age materials help in sealing leaky masonry, such as this Dow Corning Silicone Rubber Coating. It is easily applied with a conventional paint roller. (Dow Corning)

that you will find in paint stores to suit almost every conceivable wall type; some even expand to create a really solid patch in concrete walls. Leaks are another story. Have them investigated by a contractor to make sure they can be repaired inside when located below ground level. For minor seepage in porous masonry, use a sealant such as DryLok, making sure you follow instructions and clean out any crystallization prior to applying the sealer.

Floors

Check floors for water, especially around wall bases. Floors are traditional trouble spots for leaking if the exterior of your house does not drain properly. Again you may be able to solve the problem by using some of the specially formulated cement-base coatings or sealants designed to waterproof and decorate masonry or floors.

Ceilings

Check the ceiling, to make sure wood joists are sound. One way to check for dry rot or insects is to take an ice pick and push it into the wood. If the wood breaks across the grain and lifts out easily, you had better call in the experts to assure its soundness.

Assuming that your potential family room area has passed inspection with only minor repairs necessary, you are ready to proceed. But remember: you certainly want to be sure that the shell of the room is sound before investing one cent to decorate or remodel it.

Insulation

Insulation is the unsung hero in reducing your heating bill throughout your house, and is especially important in creating the proper temperature for a family room. Insulation can change a damp and clammy basement into an inviting, snug place, keep out heat in summer, or cold in the winter. With insulation you can more easily regulate the temperature and moisture level, with less strain on the heating or cooling units you use. Here are the simple steps to follow in insulating your family room.

Seal Air Leaks

These occur around window and door frames and along sill plates. Consider also any doorway that leads to an unheated area of the house, such as the basement or sunporch.

Doorways. Seal any gap that occurs in uneven spots between the top of the foundation wall and the bottom of the sill plate, using a caulking gun from the inside.

Silicone caulk and sealer provides a tough, waterproof seal even on a masonry joint. Seal air leaks wherever they occur. (Dow Corning)

Windows. These may need special attention. Windows must be double-glazed to reduce heat loss, and storm windows are a must for comfort in cold climates. A less expensive alternative, somewhat on the temporary side, is to use clear plastic sheeting stapled over the window frame or taped into place on metal frames during winter.

Weatherstripping. This keeps down the air flow around any often-used opening. Consider weatherstripping outside doors and those leading to unheated areas.

Add whatever weatherstripping is needed to doorways and windows, including prefabricated thresholds that can update older doors. Your insulation job will only be as good as the soundness of all areas, including the openings.

Insulation Materials

Types included batt or blanket, board or rigid insulation, and loose fill. The first two are the usual favorites of do-it-yourselfers, since loose fill often must be applied with a special machine for uniformity of thickness and insulation. However, loose fill sometimes is the only choice for hard-to-insulate areas, such as under the eaves.

Batts are relatively short lengths, suitable for small jobs, while blankets are rolls ready for cutting to the needed length. Both come with or without a built-in vapor barrier. Board or rigid insulation is either applied by foam or bought in sheets, and is particularly good used over smooth walls.

You cannot tell the efficiency of insulation by its thickness, since the materials that comprise it determine that. Fortunately, insulation materials are graded according to their "R-Value," which is a number given for the resistance to heat flow. The larger the R-value number, the greater the resistance or insulating properties. Suggested minimum ratings are: Ceilings, R-19; Sidewalls, R-11; floors over unheated areas, R-11; basement walls, R-7. Keep in mind that these are minimums and that the more insulation you build in, the better.

Installation

Installation methods vary slightly when you are working on the ceiling, sill header, or the walls. The

	BATTS OR BLANKETS		LOOSE FILL (POURED-IN)			
	glass fiber	rock wool	glass fiber	rock wool	cellulosic fiber	
R-11	3½"-4"	3"	5"	4"	3"	R-11
R-19	6"-6½"	5¼"	8"-9"	6"-7"	5"	R-19
R-22	6½"	6"	10"	7"-8"	6"	R-22
R-30	9½"-10½"*	9"*	13"-14"	10"-11"	8"	R-30
R-38	12"-13"*	10½"*	17"-18"	13"-14"	10"-11"	R-38

* two batts or blankets required.

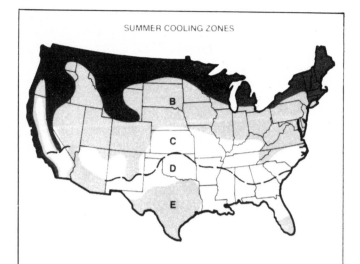

SUMMER COOLING ZONES

ATTIC INSULATION FOR SUMMER COOLING						
AIR CONDITIONING COST		RECOMMENDED INSULATION				
ELECTRIC (kWh)	GAS (therm)	ZONE A	ZONE B	ZONE C	ZONE D	ZONE E
1.5¢	9¢	—	—	—	R-11	R-11
2¢	12¢	—	—	R-11	R-11	R-11
2.5¢	15¢	—	—	R-11	R-11	R-19
3¢	18¢	—	R-11	R-11	R-11	R-19
4¢	24¢	—	R-11	R-11	R-19	R-30
5¢	30¢	—	R-11	R-19	R-19	R-30
6¢	36¢	—	R-11	R-19	R-30	R-30

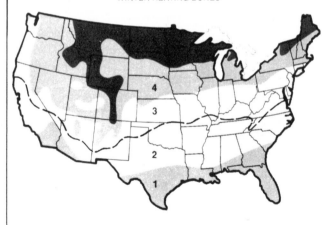

WINTER HEATING ZONES

ATTIC INSULATION FOR WINTER HEATING								
HEATING COST				RECOMMENDED INSULATION				
GAS (therm)	OIL (gallon)	ELECTRIC RESISTANCE (kWh)	ELECTRIC HEAT PUMP (kWh)	ZONE 1	ZONE 2	ZONE 3	ZONE 4	ZONE 5
9¢	13¢	—	1¢	—	R-11	R-11	R-19	R-19
12¢	17¢	—	1.3¢	—	R-11	R-19	R-19	R-30
15¢	21¢	—	1.7¢	—	R-11	R-19	R-30	R-30
18¢	25¢	1¢	2¢	—	R-11	R-19	R-30	R-30
24¢	34¢	1.3¢	2.6¢	R-11	R-19	R-30	R-33	R-38
30¢	42¢	1.6¢	3.3¢	R-11	R-19	R-30	R-33	R-38
36¢	50¢	2¢	4¢	R-11	R-30	R-33	R-38	R-44
54¢	75¢	3¢	6¢	R-11	R-30	R-38	R-49	R-49
72¢	$1.00	4¢	8¢	R-19	R-38	R-44	R-49	R-60
90¢	$1.25	5¢	10¢	R-19	R-38	R-49	R-57	R-66

single most important factor to remember is to PLACE THE VAPOR BARRIER ON THE WARM, INSIDE SIDE OF THE INSULATION. Otherwise, you run the risk of soggy insulation from the normal moisture that collects within a house.

Use basic framing with 2 x 4's spaced according to the dimensions of your insulation. These are 16 inches on center, added to the masonry walls of a basement. Insulation batts fit between studs, and paneling is easily applied to finish the walls handsomely. (Marlite Paneling)

Fiberglass insulation batts are applied by stapling to studs, with staples going through the small flange provided on either side. Always place the vapor barrier facing the room, as this foil-faced insulation illustrates. (CertainTeed insulation)

Ceilings. Insulate the ceiling of a basement family/recreation room only when you want to lower temperature there without creating coldness in the rest of the house. Another reason to insulate the ceiling is to cut down on the noise level from the family/recreation room. Without these two conditions, you may not want or need to insulate the ceiling of the basement at all. If you do decide to insulate, lay up your insulation so that the vapor barrier faces down, into the room.

Sill Headers. Insulate around the sill header, especially if you have chosen not to insulate the ceiling area. To do this, first insulate the spaces between floor joists, installing fiberglass insulation vertically with the vapor barrier facing the basement. Cut it slightly larger than the space for a tight fit. Rigid foam also can be used to insulate the sill header.

Walls. Walls below grade need moisture protection from both the inside and the outside surfaces, since some moisture is bound to seep in from the ground surrounding the walls. Here are the steps to follow in installing batts or blankets. You can use these steps, eliminating step one, when working on walls above ground level, if outside walls are in good shape.

1. If the insulation you have chosen does not have a built-in vapor barrier, cover the entire wall with 6 mil polyethylene sheet to create one. Staple it to the bottom plate and blocking strip, as well as along the furring strips. Allow an ample margin when cutting out around windows and doorways so that you can securely staple film for a good seal around such openings.

2. Make a framework to hold the insulation, consisting of wood furring strips, a blocking strip, and bottom plate. Furring should be either 2 x 2's or 2 x 4's, depending on the thickness of your insulation. Space between the vertical furring strips should fit the width of the insulation. For instance, make furring 16 inches on center for batting 16 inches wide, or 24 inches on center for batting 24 inches wide.

Secure the bottom plate to the basement floor against the foundation wall. Then, fasten the blocking strip to the sill plate or the ceiling joists. The blocking strip should be thick enough to fit between the top of the foundation and the ceiling joists, and butt against the sill plate while extending to the inner edge of the foundation wall. Then, nail furring strips to blocking plate and bottom plate, spaced according to insulation width.

3. Collect the tools needed for installing insulation. These include a razor-blade-type cutting knife, a pair of long-blade scissors, stud-height measuring stick, folding ruler, pair of step-ladders and scaffold plank for reaching the top, manual staple-gun and staples, helper's T-shaped hold-up device, gloves to protect your hands from the fiberglass. In tight spaces, you may want to add a breathing mask to be sure you do not inhale any fibers. Use electrical adhesive tape to repair cuts and tears.

4. Use your precut stud-height measuring stick to cut a number of blanket lengths at one time. Beginning at a corner, start stapling blank to furring strips or studs, every five inches. Press the fibers back from the

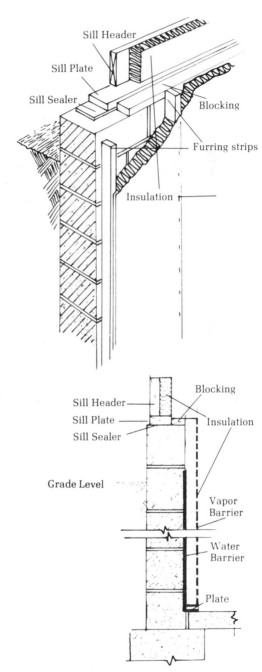

Frame for adding insulation. (Courtesy of New York State Electric & Gas Corp., Binghampton, N.Y. 13902)

barrier cover at the top and bottom, so that you can create a flange to staple to base and top plate. Allow the flanges to meet over studs, or even better, to overlap as you go from one space to another. If the insulation is thicker than the stud depth, staple flange to side of studs instead of front.

5. Repair the inevitable tears and cuts in the vapor barrier as you go along, using electrical adhesive tape. Even a small tear in the vapor barrier is enough to let in moisture that will give you soggy walls.

6. Place insulation around the back of pipes, ducts, and electrical wires and boxes instead of in front of them.

7. Fill in small areas where batts do not fit, such as around a chimney, and cut insulation to size with vapor barrier to the inside.

Heating and Ventilation

Maintaining the proper temperature and atmosphere in your family room not only insures its comfort, but protects your investment from mildew and mustiness. Depending upon the climate in your area, you may want to invest in a heating or air conditioning system, and a dehumidifier. Natural ventilation with ordinary windows will take care of most loads, but you would want ventilation for special-need areas such as a second kitchen or bath. All of these considerations are just that much more important when the family/recreation room is in an enclosed basement.

Heating

Your requirements may involve a mere tapping into the existing system used for the rest of the house. Local building codes may come into play with the additional work necessary to tap into your present system, and to create the duct work to expand it to the family room area. For this reason, it is a good idea to call in a subcontractor. Overloading your existing facility will not only prove inadequate for the new family room, it will also bring down the efficiency of your heating in the rest of the house. However, there are other solutions should you need to add supplementary heating. (See "Fireplaces and Stoves" later in this chapter).

Ductwork. The ductwork is done before any plumbing or electrical work, because duct parts take considerably more space between the studs and joists, so should be fitted first. Plan the outlets for ducts to provide even heating throughout the room, and to work conveniently with your furniture arrangements. For instance, avoid a duct opening where you plan to place either a game table or built-in sofa.

Hot water heat without plumbing is provided with electric baseboard heaters that have a system complete within themselves. Lightweight units plug into any 110-120 volt electric outlet, are automatically controlled by a built-in thermostat. (Intertherm Inc.)

Electrical baseboards. These are a good alternate choice when the heating of additional space would place an overload on your heating plant. There are special units designed for many situations, such as wall units for small spaces like baths, kitchen areas or entranceways; recessed units to use before sliding doors and floor-length windows; and traditional baseboard designs of varying lengths. A closed water system is used in some of these to spread the heat throughout the room, without the need of a water hookup.

Air Conditioning

Air conditioning not only cools, but removes humidity. You may be able to use the central air conditioning from the rest of the house; if this is not feasible, take a look at the room-sized air conditioners that are scaled in capacity for your family room space.

Wiring. Wiring to accommodate your air conditioning should be installed in the beginning if not already incorporated, and should be positioned where the unit will go.

Efficiency. Air-conditioner efficiency has improved over recent years, although the most efficient units are still at the top of the price scale. Since the most efficient units use the least electricity to cool the same space as their less competent, less expensive competitors, you would often spread out the cost of the better unit within a few years through saved electrical costs.

Keep in mind that you want a unit of the proper capacity for your total space. A too-small unit that overworks is bound to show wear and become less efficient in a shorter time. Conversely, you will waste electricity by buying a unit designed to cool an area much larger than that at hand. Your air conditioner dealer can give you the efficiency ratings and whatever guarantees or warranties are available on current air conditioning models. It is a good idea to check out the servicing plans for any air conditioner you buy.

Another factor in choosing an air conditioning unit is how it will look. You may wish to install a unit through the wall rather than taking up window space in the room. Most units are designed to be discreet additions that do not interfere with the design of a room, while others may have styling that will coordinate with your cabinetry.

Dehumidifiers

Dehumidifiers have saved many basements converted into family rooms, since the cold moist air from throughout the house tends to collect at this lowest point. A dehumidifier helps reduce moisture content and protect wood and other contents from warping,

Through-the-wall air conditioners are more attractive than window models. They are installed using a metal sleeve that is attached to a framed-in wall opening. Provide an electric outlet nearby, and adjust unit permanently after wall is completed. (Hotpoint Conditioner)

rust, and mildew. Make sure your humidifier is the right capacity for the room. A number of dehumidifiers are styled to look like attractive cabinets, with wood-grain finishes to coordinate with furniture styles.

"RATING" YOUR ELECTRIC EQUIPMENT

Obviously, on all your electrical purchases you will want to get as high an Energy Efficiency Ratio (EER) as you can. Usually the EER rating is attached to the new appliances as well as being stamped on the metal plate of air conditioners. The higher the operating efficiency the higher the number attached to EER, and the less expensive it will be for you to operate. If the wattage of the unit is not listed on the item, you can find it quickly by multiplying the listed amperes by the voltage the unit operates on, either 120 or 240 volts. Thus 10 amperes times 120 volts equals 1,200 watts. An EER of 10 is great; 8 to 9 is good; 6 to 7 is passable. An appliance with an EER rating of 8.8, as compared to one that rates 6.3, would cost you about 28 percent less on your bill.

Ventilation

Consider ventilation at the same time you are undertaking duct work for heating, since the ducts are similar. You may be able to consolidate the ductwork and ventilation from the kitchen, laundry, and bath areas into one plan. Basically, any high-moisture-producing activity calls for an exhaust ventilator going directly to the outside or ducted to it. The closer to the outside of the wall, the more efficient the exhaust unit will be, so keep this in mind when planning locations of your high-moisture areas.

Ducts can be used to bring moisture to outside walls from almost any area if need be, with fans installed near the moisture source. Regular rectangular duct sections ordinarily used for heating systems can be used, but if space demands, you also can employ flexible ducts that snake around structural members and other obstructions.

Johns-Manville makes such flexible round metal air duct material, which requires no extra joints or special fittings, and can be installed through the roof with a cap, through the wall with an outside wall cap, through an outside soffit, or even vented through a louvered vent and snaked through the upper floor.

Since moisture is a major problem in basements, the use of vents is most crucial. But, a good vent will save in wear and tear and need for cleaning of any family room, no matter where its location. Vents allow air-borne grease and soil as well as moisture to go straight outdoors without settling on furniture and draperies.

Plumbing

Family/recreation room plumbing needs generally include a bath of some sort and a food-serving area. How extensive you want to make either unit is strictly a matter of choice. In either case, the basic plumbing must be installed before any finishing work.

Local building codes are always the last word when it comes to proper plumbing, and local contractors and plumbers are well-versed with the specifications in your area. You can sometimes work out an arrangement with a plumber where you assist and save some of the expenses, while taking advantage of his expertise. You will need good advice, especially for installing waste disposal plumbing below-ground to achieve the proper vapor lock or release. This is necessary to insure that you have no backwash that might contaminate a fresh water supply. Most professionals can recommend units especially designed for use below-grade.

This sauna comes in a kit that includes everything needed to custom install a luxurious, two-person sauna in almost any closet-sized space. Included is a door that has controls, light, heater, and ventilation. It runs on standard household current. (Viking Custom Duo Sauna Kit)

Tiles have finally become easy to install, thanks to the Redi-Set sheets now available. Sheets are factory grouted with flexible, non-cracking silicone rubber which resists stains and mildew. Joints are filled with a hand gun using matching grout. (American Olean)

Bathrooms. It can be as limited as a half-bath, or as complex as units with a sauna or steam room. If you think you might want to install an elaborate unit some time in the future, plan your layout for the bath, the wiring and plumbing lines that will be required, so these can be installed now. Then you need only hook up the additional units you need when the time comes.

Family room baths can include merely a toilet and sink; however, expanded units enable this room to take over the family bathroom congestion overload. For instance, you might want to add an all-in-one shower stall. If you are an avid planter, you might also want to add a good potting sink. Or, you might want to keep this room as a sort of extended mud room, where you can clean up completely after gardening or sunning, without having to traipse through the house.

Universal-Rundle's Mediterranean style vanity is shown here with the firm's 24-inch drop-on cultured marble bowl top. The white-on-white unit has a raised soap dish that swirls into the bowl.

Offered in 12 colors, American-Standard's Oval Contura (left below) is a lightweight plastic lavatory said to be chip free, stain resistant and rustproof. It comes with 4 or 8 inch centers, measures 20 x 17 inches and has a depth of 6⅛ inches.

Designated the Man's Lav by Kohler (right below), this 28 x 19-inch cast iron fixture has built-in dispenser for soap or lotion and spray shampoo fitting in addition to conventional water controls and faucet. The self-rimming lavatory is installed here in a plastic laminate countertop.

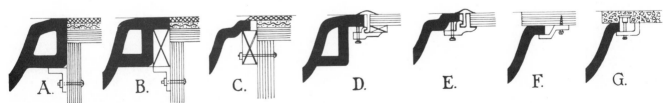

RECESSING A LAVATORY can be accomplished by various means depending upon the type of countertop selected. Diagrams A, B and C show lavatory bowls joined with ceramic tile countertops; D, E and F are set in decorative plastic laminate; G is set in marble.

Kitchens. Requirements include adequate plumbing and wiring. The aforementioned planting center can be incorporated into a family room miniature kitchen area, providing you have specified a large-enough sink and proper drain area. Consider all of the potential uses for the kitchen area when putting in the plumbing and wiring.

Wiring

Local building codes are key factors in the suitable installation of wiring for both lighting and other uses. While you may find the codes overly scrupulous, keep in mind that they are all designed to save you from dire consequences, such as fire. And since the contractors in your area are well versed in specific local codes, have them work out and install the system you need unless you are very handy. Make sure that any subcontracting you do specifies compliance with local codes in the contract.

Estimate the amount of electricity you will need, based on your planned activities in the family room. List such basics as lighting, kitchen appliances, air conditioning, heating, stereo, and television. Then, add the special equipment that is unique to your interests. For instance, you might want to install an elaborate amplification system for sound, or require heavy-duty lines for a woodworking center.

Since electrical needs for various products seem to increase yearly, make sure your overall plan allows for future loads. You will also want to distribute your loads over at least two circuits and separate major lighting into two circuits. This way, you run less risk of blowing the fuses or tripping a circuit breaker, and will also have one lighted circuit going even if the other blows. In an enclosed basement, lighting is a very important consideration.

If you decide to handle some of the wiring yourself, be absolutely sure that the work does comply with national and local building codes. And, follow all safety procedures, including proper grounding of any wires.

Grounded

The current-carrying conductor in your electrical service box that has a white or neutral grey color is a neutral conductor. It runs through the circuitry, back through the distribution panel and perhaps to the service entrance, to be attached to a single system ground. This may be provided by a clamp on the cold-water main-supply line that comes up from beneath the ground. Or, in some cases, it may be connected to an outdoor ground pipe driven adjacent to the meter location. This is a "grounded" system.

Ground fault interrupter is combined with a duplex convenience outlet in this Leviton-made device which should be used for outdoor outlets, and in other hazardous locations where the entire circuit is not protected by a GFT-type breaker at the circuit distribution panel. The interrupter is sensitive to leaking current, protecting against the possibility of serious shocks. It includes a test button to verify proper operating condition.

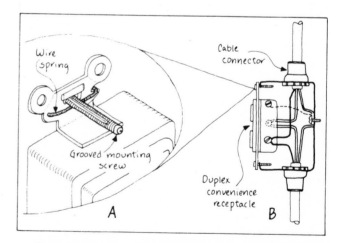

Receptacle Grounding Detail indicates two methods of providing adequate electrical bonding of the switch or outlet receptacle to the electrical box to maintain grounding continuity. In sketch (A), a built-in wire spring is provided in some devices so proper box contact is made when the device is screwed to the box. In sketch (B), an alternative method. The dashed line rperesentes a bonding jumper wire from the bonding screw terminal to the box ground screw. The National Electrical Code requires bonding of all electrical system enclosures such as raceways, cable armor, cable sheath, frames, fittings and noncurrent-carrying metal parts.

Grounding

In addition to a "grounded" system, building codes require an emergency "grounding" of all electrical system enclosures, boxes, switches, receptacles, and lighting-fixture metal parts. This is accomplished by clipping or screwing grounding wires to outlet boxes.

Ground Fault Interrupter

In 1975 a series of revisions in the National Electrical Code initiated new requirements for residential electrical systems and their use of grounding outlet receptacles. Although the grounding system, evidenced by the use of 3-hole receptacles for 3-prong plugs, gave protection to circuits and appliances in the case of serious shorts or overloads, it was still possible for electric currents to leak to the grounding channel in small amounts that were insufficient to set off the protective breakers, but sufficient to cause serious shocks. The grounding system did not protect people who touched parts of outlet boxes, tools, or equipment that had grounding leakage.

A device called the "ground fault interrupter" was developed to counter this hazard. It monitors the grounding circuit, and when it detects any small flow of current in the range between 5 and 15 milliamperes, it interrupts the circuit and shuts off the circuit. A person who touches such a faulty grounding part or lid may receive a direct flow of this small current to ground through his body. The victim will receive an initial shock, but the interrupter operates within $1/40$ of a second; he will be able to free himself and thus avoid a possibly otherwise fatal shock.

Insuring Adequate Wiring

In addition to planning the placement of major appliances, plan outlets for lamps and small electrical accessories so that each area will be easily serviced. You are better off with an unused wall socket than in having to resort to extension cords.

Lighting

Consider all your lighting needs when planning the wiring of your family room. You will want to use the three main types of lighting: general, local, and accent or dramatic lighting.

General

General lighting lightens up dark corners and provides an attractive field of light throughout the room. Good general lighting is especially important for dark rooms without much sunlight, and for rooms used often at night. Recessed ceiling panels are designed to give general lighting, and are favorite choices for family rooms since they are relatively easy to install as part of a ceiling paneling system.

Other means of achieving general lighting are through the use of structural light fixtures that bounce light off walls or ceilings, diffusing it to brighten the entire room. Examples include valances for draperies with a built-in lighting unit, brackets placed above a sofa with light directed to the ceiling, cornices slanted and positioned close to the ceiling with light directed upward, or coves positioned near the ceiling with light sweeping downward on the wall. A series of recessed ceiling lights that spread light instead of spotlighting can also provide general lighting.

Specific Visual Task	Lumens
Reading and writing: handwriting, indistinct print, or poor copies	70
Books, magazines, newspapers	30
Music scores, advanced	70
Music scores, simple	30
Studying at desk	70
Recreation: Playing cards, billiards	30
Table tennis	20
Grooming: Shaving, combing hair, applying makeup	50
Kitchen work: At sink	70
At range	50
At work counters	50
Laundering jobs: At washer	50
At ironing board	50
At ironer	50
Sewing: Dark fabrics (fine detail, low contrast)	200
Prolonged periods (light to medium fabrics)	100
Occasional (light-colored fabrics)	50
Occasional (coarse thread, large stitched, high contrast of thread to fabric)	30
Handicraft: Close work (reading diagrams and blueprints, fine finishing)	100
Cabinet making, planing, sanding, glueing	50
Measuring, sawing, assembling, repairing	50
Any area involving a visual task	30
For safety in passage areas	10
Areas used mostly for relaxation, recreation and conversation	10

Local

Local lighting is the most important consideration for the safe and healthful pursuit of hobbies and activities. Local lighting can come from free-standing lamps or built-in lighting, so long as the appropriate amount of light for the job is provided. For instance, you would want good local lighting for either sewing or reading; local lights to illuminate musical scores placed over a piano; good local lighting to work on heavy wood-working or miniature crewelwork.

One important factor in placing good local lighting is that it be positioned properly for the user. Avoid both shadows and glare on the working surface to be illuminated. Wall-hung lamps, either free or built-in, provide good shadow-free lighting for worktables pulled to the wall. Reading lamps should be to the side and behind the users, and all lamps should be positioned so that the bulbs do not glare into the eyes of the user.

Put utility first when choosing good local lighting, although the selection of lamps can add greatly to the overall beauty of your room. Be sure the lamp you choose is suited to its location and to the job it needs to do. And remember that three-way bulb lamps can be lowered for atmosphere during conversation, and turned up for healthy eye-saving reading or sewing.

Track lights suspended above the sofa provide perfect illumination for the posters displayed on the wall. They also lighten corners and give focus to the put-together seating. (Stratford furniture)

Shades of Sidney Greenstreet are echoed with this fanciful combination light and ceiling fan. Brass holds real wood blades that quietly circulate air at two speeds. (Hunter Division Robbins & Myers, Inc.)

Accent Lighting

Accent lighting adds to the total lighting of the room, but its main function is to provide sparkle. Accent lights can be pin-dot recessed ceiling lights, soft built-in valance lights that light up draperies to life, or wildly modern sculptural lamps that offer little in light efficiency but a great deal in visual impact. Unless an accent light is used for its own intrinsic beauty, it is usually used to spotlight some section or object that needs visual reinforcement. One recent addition to the accent light field are bullet lamps that can be rotated at will to spotlight whatever objects you choose, either installed in ceiling tracks, on walls, or on the floor.

Incandescent and Fluorescent

Types of lighting fall into two categories, incandescent and fluorescent. Incandescent lighting is closest to the flattering quality of candlelight, and is generally warm and inviting. It is most often used in free-standing units. Fluorescent lighting, in contrast to incandescent light, gives off far less heat. It is the favorite for recessed or enclosed fixtures, since there is so little heat buildup and units are less costly to operate for the same amount of wattage as offered by incandescent lights.

You can buy bulbs that vary from warm to cool hues in both types of light, to get just the effects you want. You might favor cool fluorescent lights in enclosed spaces that tend to heat up; the new warmwhites will give flattering light and still give the savings of fluorescents. Or, use incandescent lights to add warmth to a large room.

Pendant lamps take up no table space and provide dramatic tabletop lighting. Gleaming brass highlights this unit with chain and mounting hardware that has a glass globe. (Stiffel lamps)

Lumen outputs of standard and long-life incandescent bulbs				
	Watts	*Lumens*	*Bulb life (hrs)*	*Lumens/watt*
Standard bulbs	100	1740	750	17.4
	75	1180	750	15.7
Long-life bulbs	100	1690	1150	16.9
	100	1490	2500	14.9
	100	1470	3000	14.7
	92	1490	2500	16.2
	90	1290	3500	14.3

A classic ginger-jar shaped table lamp goes with almost any kind of decorating style you might have chosen for your family room. The age-old shape looks well with contemporary furniture as well as antique. Gold accents the creamy china of the base. (Stiffel lamps)

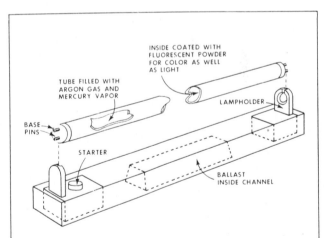

The fluorescent phosphor coating on the inside of the tube is activated by electric energy passing through the tube; light is given off. The starter in standard starter-type fixtures permits preheating of the electrodes in the ends of the tube to make it easier to start. The ballast limits the current to keep the tube functioning properly. The channel holds ballast and wiring and spaces the lampholders.

(Dept. of Agriculture).

69

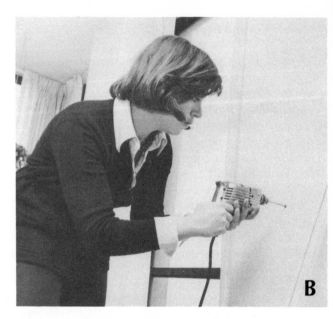

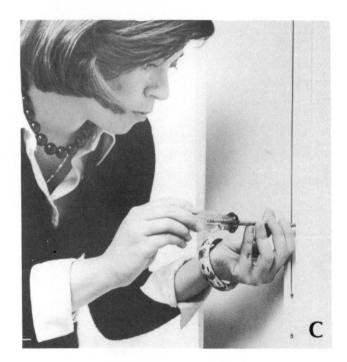

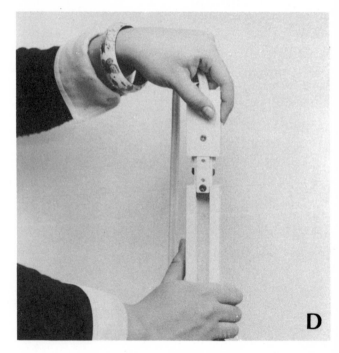

Install track lighting in five steps. (A) Place track on wall and mark fastening positions. (B) Drill holes. (C) Fasten track to wall with screws from kit. (D) Insert cord and plug connecter. (E) Once lamps are placed in the track, insert bulbs. (Halo Lighting).

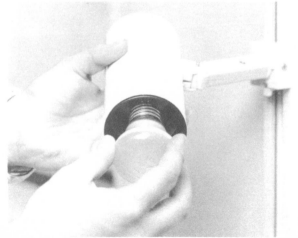

Fireplaces and Stoves

Fireplaces are so romantic and beautiful that their utility seems almost secondary, but both factors are what make them great favorites for family/recreation rooms. Manufactured, insulated chimneys make possible their installation in even the remotest areas. Free-standing units do away with most construction requirements or complications.

Factory-built fireplaces and chimneys are relatively low in cost, easy to install, and engineered for safety and good function. Some include a heat recirculating system that returns heat into the room rather than allowing it to go up the chimney. Most models have heat-shield kits that can be installed to allow you to place them near combustible walls without danger. The hearth is another part of the fireplace that is essential to its safe use. Through decorating the surround of a built-in prefabricated fireplace box or choosing a free-standing model, you can match your fireplace to the overall look of your family room.

Stoves also come under the scrutiny of Underwriter's Laboratories for safety in burning and stability from tipping. They are popular choices for more casual family rooms, in styles ranging from the well-designed Franklin stoves to contemporary models.

Here are some of the decorating considerations to make the fireplace you choose best suit your family room.

- Be sure you can arrange your furniture to take full advantage of the fireplace view. A corner unit, built out into the room to provide a view from both the front and the side, may solve seating and viewing problems.

- Consider an installation that is set in the corner of the room kitty-corner to give a wide view.

- Elevated hearths bring the fire up to eye level, and afford extra seating when extended to flank the fireplace on either side.

- Circular and two-sided fireplaces offer an exciting view from many directions. These might be a good addition for a divider of a family/kitchen area.

- Check that a stove does not have to have the front doors closed to operate efficiently, if you really want to watch the flames.

- Do not skimp on fireplace accessories such as adequate screens and tools, since they are your first line of defense when a fire starts to go out of control.

This corner fireplace gives a full view to both sides of the room, and determined the furniture arrangement. It is faced in flagstone. The flagstone color is echoed in the Custom Travertine vinyl asbestos tile color. (Azrock Floor Products)

Factory-built fireplaces with zero-clearance so that they can go right up to the wall permit the kind of facing treatments that make them look built in, and can be installed at about one-half the cost of conventional masonry units. (Heatilator fireplace)

The clean lines of this free-standing fireplace keep it from conflicting with a good view. Furniture can be arranged for both fire watching and taking in the outdoor vista. (Majestic fireplace)

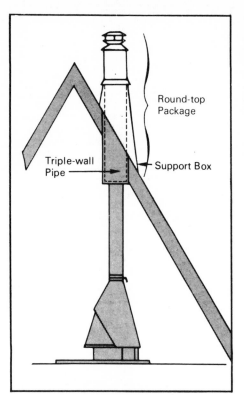

A-frame roofs pose no installation problems with the proper chimney package.

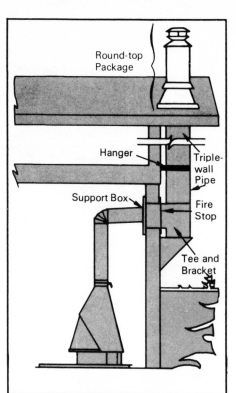

No need to cut through the attic. It's easy to elbow through an outside wall and vent straight up, using Tee and Bracket.

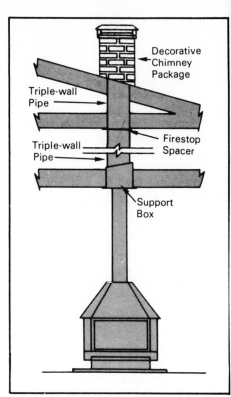

First floor installation in a two-story house. Chimney can be concealed in a second story closet.

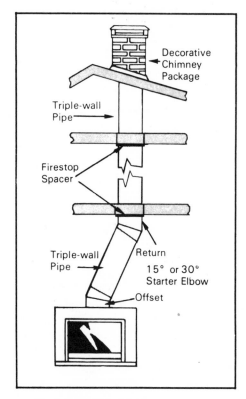

Preway chimneys clear upstairs obstructions with 15° or 30° elbows (all elbow kits include offset and return).

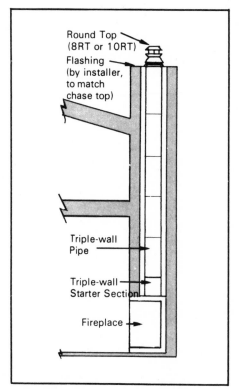

Today's space saving chase installations are a natural with Preway built-in fireplaces and chimney system.

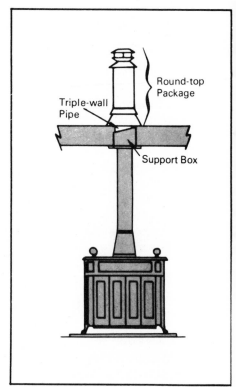

Installation through a flat roof is simple and the most economical of all.

Both fireplaces and wood burning stoves can be installed in a variety of ways: The six illustrations here detail some typical methods of chimney installation (photo courtesy of Preway).

Some manufacturers sell a heat circulator which fits into the flue and cycles air that would normally go up the chimney. (photo courtesy of Calcinator Corp.)

• Treat your fireplace or stove with the decorating respect it deserves, and expand its impact with the use of accessories above and around it.

• Include in your plans provision for the coal or wood that will be stored nearby for convenience. You can build in wood storage areas, or choose from a range of highly decorative free-standing units designed for the purpose.

• Install your fireplace unit before finishing walls or floors, so that these areas are not ruined through the addition of this object.

Local building codes govern the minimum requirements for safe installation of fireplaces or stoves, and many of the units are under the Underwriters Laboratories' fireplace-testing program. Safety factors and specifications are readily available from the manufacturers of component parts or entire fireplace units. (Technicalities of fireplace installation are covered in the *Book of Successful Fireplaces* by R. J. Lytle, listed in the Appendix.)

Heat-circulating fireplaces have intake and outtake grilles and ducts strategically placed to project warmed air from the fireplace, vastly improving fireplace efficiency. (photo courtesy of Majestic)

Stairways

Family/recreation rooms in basements are often serviced by rather temporary stairways. The added traffic and increased usage of the staircase may make its replacement necessary. For one thing, you may want to widen it to handle the materials used in remodeling the family room. And, if your plan includes a workshop, you want to be sure you can get large pieces down the stairs.

Provide lights at the top and bottom of the stairs with independent switches on either floor, and arrange the stairway so that it works well with the design of the room below. Corner staircases, circular staircases, and straight staircases are all available in prefabricated parts that assure their strength and comfortable dimensions for going up and down.

You can totally enclose a staircase, provide a half-partition so that those coming into the family room have a view of it from the upper half of the stair, or use an open staircase. All are attractive and efficient.

Side-opening fireplaces are the perfect answer for certain room arrangements. Who would want to miss the view when this solution allows clear vision from two angles. Firebox and chimney components have triple-wall construction, allowing any framing and trim. (photo courtesy of Majestic)

HOW TO BUILD AND FRAME PARTITIONS

A room or area may be divided or changed in shape by the construction of a simple nonbearing partition. Because nonbearing partitions do not support the floor above, their construction is lighter and easier than that of load-bearing partitions.

Nonbearing partitions generally are constructed of 2x4-inch studs, set either 16 or 24 inches apart. The bottom of the studs are nailed to another 2x4 called the sole plate, which is nailed to the floor. A top plate, also 2x4, is nailed to the ceiling, or in the case of an unfinished basement or attic, directly to the ceiling joists or rafters.

To align the new partition, measure its location from an existing wall and then, using a chalk line (1) mark a straight line on the floor. The partition sole plate is then set against the chalk line (2) and nailed to the floor.

Using a level to insure the partition being level, (3) nail the first studs to the existing walls. Once these end studs are in place, set the top plate (4) by nailing it to the bottom of the ceiling joists or the ceiling. Place the studs on 16-inch (or 24-inch) centers and toenail (5) them on both sides to both the sole plate and the top plate.

Where ceiling heights and clearances permit, it is possible to assemble the partition on the floor and then tilt it into place. Studs should be doubled at the sides and tops of all openings, and never be notched (for wires, pipes, etc.) more than one-third their depth (Photos: Georgia-Pacific Corporation).

"Olde Amsterdam" patterned resilient sheet flooring hides seams once they have been joined. A sheepskin area rug can be moved into position wherever needed as the furniture is rearranged for various activities. (Armstrong flooring)

6. Flooring Lays the Groundwork

The main choices for family room floors are carpeting, sheet resilient flooring, hard flooring, or tile applications of some of the above. Each offers its own unique decorative advantages, and can be chosen in dramatic patterns and color, or subtle, subdued versions.

Your first decision is whether to make the floor covering dominant within the room, or to act as an understatement. If your furniture arrangement allows for constant rearranging, you might want to keep the furniture subtle, and allow the flooring to carry the decorative load. In this way, each arrangement will look well wherever it is placed, and you will not change the decorative emphasis by changing the furniture placement.

Another good reason for using a dominant flooring is to help unify a large expanse of space. Good choices in this case would be large, bold patterns, to minimize the scale of the room. In the same way, a definite directional pattern might help bring an awkwardly shaped room into better proportion. For instance, a resilient flooring that has a striped effect running across a narrow room will make that room seem wider.

Finally, the awkwardly shaped room with many cut-up spaces can be unified with a lively floor treatment. In this case, you might want to minimize the walls through a subtle, receding and monotone treatment, so that room will need the added zip of interest underfoot.

In contrast, if your walls are to be the dominant expanses within the room, you will want to tone down the floor. Even with one focus wall, such as the fireplace wall, make sure that the decorative thrust of the area is not placed in conflict with an overly decorative floor treatment.

For a feeling of serenity, consider using the same colors, perhaps in varying hues, for the walls and floors. With a focal wall, or a particularly dominant furniture grouping, coordinating the major surfaces in this fashion will make the room seem larger. It also helps the focus of the room stand out better.

One final point to remember in selecting the right floor covering is its cleaning ease and ability to mask soil.

Carpeting

Carpeting is an elegant choice for family rooms that have no pretentions as game rooms. The use of warm woven material on the floor gives an intimacy to the room that no other floor covering can quite match. While obviously not the best choice if you anticipate extreme roughhousing or real messiness, carpeting cleaning today is so easy with new fabrics, that it is a good choice for many all-purpose family rooms.

If children will end up playing on the floor, give real thought to installing carpeting. When their play pattern does not include spills, you might even find that the quick vacuuming necessary to keep a carpet in good shape is easier than the care required for wood or resilient floors.

Selection

The quality pointers in buying long-lasting carpeting include the pile height, density of the pile, and toughness of the fibers. The pile, or front face of the carpeting, can have yarns that are relatively long as in shag rug, medium height as in a loose plush, or short as in a velvet. Variations in the surface include cutting the loops of the pile, leaving it uncut, or using a combination of both. Generally, the uncut loop carpets are the longest wearing.

The second consideration is the density of the pile, or how much fabric is actually used on the surface. One way of judging this is to fold back carpeting samples, and compare the amount of bald space between tufts from one piece to another. The thicker the pile, the longer the good looks of the carpet will last, as a general rule.

Both of the above factors affect the amount of tracking that a carpet will show over the years. Denser, tighter piles show paths of wear much less than do their looser, longer counterparts. Sacrifice the luxurious look for your family room in favor of the all-purpose utility of tighter constructions for the greatest longevity of the carpeting.

Finally, the fiber used in the carpeting is another factor in its quality. Modern fibers such as nylon acrylic, olefin, polypropylene and polyester com-

This shag has both cut and looped face fibers, giving even more textural interest than would a cut shag. The combination of fiber colors is a good bet for hiding soil, although the stain-resistant nylon yarns used keep the carpet clean a long time. (Armstrong "Country Hearth")

The lines in the plaid help expand the visual area of this room. You can use the visual pattern of any flooring to expand a room, or to make it seem more cosy. The handsome pattern is called "Ferguson", and comes in a number of colors in Anso nylon fiber. (Allied Chemical)

A medium-toned heavy plush carpet in a solid color is a good choice with furniture that is highly patterned. This one, called "Stardom," is made of Trevira stain-resistant fibers. (Hoechst Fibers)

Here is an overall pattern that has some Art Deco feeling in "Orly" design. It works well with fine furniture pieces, without overwhelming them. ("Wishes" carpet collection from Armstrong)

pete with the ever-popular wool. Technology by the fiber manufacturers has improved the fibers used in carpeting.

Shop around to see which fiber suits your needs and pocketbook. Carpeting retailers will give you literature on current styles, and bring you up to date on the qualities of the fibers.

Ask about stain resistance, ease of cleaning, crush and abrasion resistance, and general resilience. The latter assures that the carpeting bounces back without leaving spots where furniture or people have stood.

Your lending institution may also want to make sure that the carpeting you choose meets current standards, particularly those specified by the FHA. Wall-to-wall carpeting is a considerable investment, but it also enhances the value of the completed job. As a general rule, your best economy is to start with quality. By the time you add the cost of two installations with cheaper carpeting that will wear out sooner, the more expensive carpeting that lasts twice as long becomes the best buy.

Hardly dramatic but equally important is the cushioning that you use for your carpeting. If your family room is in an area that is prone to moisture, you can benefit from the new synthetics. These will resist mold and mildew, the banes of many basement family rooms.

Backing or cushioning saves on the wear of the carpeting, and also adds a luxurious feeling underfoot that no carpeting alone can give. Some of the new synthetic carpetings come with pre-applied foam-backing, saving in installation costs. Discuss with your retailer which type would work best in your specific family room.

Installation

If you choose carpeting over a separate padding, you might need the services of the installer. Even slight bulges will cause wear on the carpet, as well as poor appearance. If the retailer who sells the carpet does not have an installation service, ask for recommendations. But usually all the aspects of the job will be handled by the same company.

One alternative is the use of cushion-backed carpeting usable by the do-it-yourselfer. The tacking method used by professionals is best if strenuous play is likely to dislodge the carpeting. With less active usage, a foam-backed carpeting will stay in place even without tacking, once you have positioned it. Tape or carpet adhesive anchors the edges and whatever seams are necessary, in this form of installation. You will need the help of friends to properly position and secure the carpeting, and then can follow the manufacturer's suggestions on securing it permanently.

Measuring

Measuring and estimating carpeting are the two most important factors in getting the most for your money. When two pieces are seamed, the carpeting should go in the same direction. Otherwise, the two pieces will not seem to match, since the reflection off the surfaces will vary slightly. Standard carpeting bolts are 12 and 15 feet wide, which is the basic measure that will work in your measuring and calculating estimates.

Invariably, you will lose some yardage in the process of matching. The trick is to try different arrangements so that you come up with the one that is most economical. For instance, in a room that measures 17 by 22 feet, the best arrangement would be to use two 12 foot widths crosswise with a seam in the center. You will have extra carpeting of 2 feet along one short end of the room. At first glance, you might make the mistake of ordering a 15 foot width, and run it the long way for 22 feet. But, you would have to buy an additional roll length (12 or 15 feet wide), to get the added two foot strip along the side, and to have it going in the same direction.

It goes without saying that checking and double checking is really important before finalizing your carpeting order, because once it is cut, you own it. So ask the carpeting retailer to double check with you unless you are totally sure that you know exactly what, where, and how the carpeting is to finally be used.

Rugs

Technically, anything which is not wall-to-wall is a rug, and calls for some finishing around the outer edges. Rugs also need good cushioning to extend their life, and to protect against slipping and sliding.

Almost-room-sized rugs are one way of handling the wall-to-wall look, but without the need to fit the carpeting to exact specifications. By leaving an exposed edge around your walls, you will make an overly large room seem smaller.

There are practical considerations in opting for an almost-room-sized rug. For one, it can be stored during the summer, giving your family room an entirely new, cooler look. Secondly, you may be able to find a large-sized remnant that is considerably less than the cost of installing wall-to-wall, exact-fit carpeting. And, if your room is symmetrical, you can minimize the wear on the rug by reversing it so that different areas receive the heaviest traffic.

Area rugs serve mainly as decorative accents, since the rest of the flooring will be visible. These are not recommended for rooms where children constantly play, unless the rugs are well out of the traffic area. The obvious danger is tripping or slipping.

Accent or area rugs are wonderful decorative accents for conversational groupings, such as those placed before the sofa and under the coffee table. They soften and warm up seating arrangements, and make them doubly inviting.

Consider the addition of such a rug if the main area of your family room should be left bare (as it might be if dancing is a favorite occupation, or if somewhat messy activities such as painting are to take place in part of the space). Accent rugs serve to unify small spaces, and at the same time set them off in a very special way.

Accent rugs can be chosen to reflect the colors of the furniture or other dominant pieces in the room, or to act as subtle backgrounds for special pieces. For

Sculptured shag carpet squares have dense foam rubber backing, with self-stick on the back for easy application over existing floor surface. These carpet squares show no seams in wall-to-wall installation. (Photo courtesy of Armstrong Cork Company)

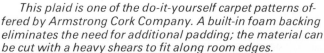

This plaid is one of the do-it-yourself carpet patterns offered by Armstrong Cork Company. A built-in foam backing eliminates the need for additional padding; the material can be cut with a heavy shears to fit along room edges.

Rugs can go directly on the floor, or be used to accent areas on top of wall-to-wall carpeting, as illustrated here. The recliners- and love-seat patterns look best on the solid color, while the traditional braid rug adds a more traditional touch. (Berkline furniture)

A natural fur rug is an opulent accent to a beautiful floor, and serves to set off the coffee table and seating area as well. A floor as pretty as this one deserves to be shown. (Parquet blocks in Heritage Square by Bruce Hardwood Flooring)

A wildly bright and colorful contemporary rug serves as the color scheme source for this entire room. Gold and to-mato red are the dominant colors, in deep shag. ("Lofoten" by Ege Rya, Inc.)

instance, a beautiful sculptured coffee table in a dark wood might need visual separation from a dark floor; a light-colored accent rug would be perfect. Or, the accent rug itself might become the theme for upholstery colors used in a grouping of chairs around it.

There are many delightful accent rug patterns and styles to choose from, and even kits for making them yourself. Examples are simulated animal skins, elegant Orientals, Navajo Indian rugs, woven seisal primitives, and a whole raft of contemporary styles. In fact, accent rugs are so handsome that they are often used as artworks on walls.

A rule of thumb in choosing the rug size to work with your furniture arrangements is to place all the furniture either off the rug or on it. That is, a small accent rug should not be partly under the sofa and coffee table, with adjoining chairs totally off the rug. In this case, choose a rug that is just large enough to rest under the coffee table and come up to the sofa and chair front legs. Or, extend the area rug totally beneath any adjoining furniture.

You can make your own decorative accent rugs by buying small remnants of carpeting and hemming them yourself with fringe. The carpet tapes that are used for hemming makes this job simpler than you might think. Just study the methods used to attach the professional fringes, and modify them to suit your own remnants. If you want to take on more of a challenge, create your own rug patterns by sewing or taping together small remnants of various colors and similar height in an effective crazy-quilt, checkerboard pattern, or any other design you develop.

Whether your area rug is a homemade master-piece or designed by a manufacturer, remember to keep it well groomed. Rotate it to keep the wear pattern dispersed, especially if it is placed in the high-traffic area in front of a sofa. And clean it as frequently as needed.

Sheet Resilient Flooring

Sheet resilient flooring is smooth-surface flooring that can be anything from hard and shiny to soft, cushioned, and matte-finished. Dimensional effects are used to create patterns that give a feeling of depth and texture. Virtually any kind of pattern is available in either tile or sheet. Some of the most popular simulate decorative tiles, natural-look materials such as wood flooring, brick, slate, or unglazed tiles, plus an entire range of solids and patterns.

You cheat yourself if you do not investigate the advantages of the newer, no-wax, and stain-resistant resilient floorings available today. You need not spend much time at all in maintaining these elegant floor coverings, and they stay as decorative as when you first installed them. Vinyl virtually dominates the resilient flooring market, largely due to major advances in easy care and styling, made through technological improvements.

Practical considerations as well as aesthetics determine whether resilient flooring is for you. You may find it cheapest to restain or paint an existing wood floor to give it a festive look, rather than investing in a new floor covering. Or, you might decide that the warmth and coziness that is missing in your family room plan will be instantly added through carpeting. But, in many cases, you'll decide that resilient flooring is the best of all possible answers for your family room, once you have seen the wide variety of patterns and looks available.

One important consideration is which of the products is suited to the floor to be covered. Ask your retailer about this, and check with the manufacturer's literature. Some floor coverings are not recommended for application to basement, lower-level or porch concrete floors, since they do not work well when applied directly to slabs-on-ground or below grade. Others may have a special preparation procedure that adapts them to such use.

In any case, your best application is going to be over a surface free from ridges or hollows, of relatively uniform smoothness. Any wood-plywood-underlayment surface that has these properties will take to resilient floor covering admirably.

Resilience of the flooring is a plus when it comes to foot fatigue, and a feeling of general comfort. Cushioning is a blessing in an area where you're likely to remain standing for long periods of time, as you might in a workshop area. On the other hand, you'll want to protect a highly cushioned area from furniture dents through the use of coasters. As with carpeting, satisfy your own tastes as to when a bouncy cushioning underfoot is too springy.

Tougher, harder surfaces might be the best choice for playroom areas where an absolutely flat flooring

Tile motifs are favorites in sheet resilient flooring, and the exuberant pattern called pattern called "Espana" in cushioned vinyl shows why. Seams are invisible, although width is only 6 feet for easy handling. (Congoleum flooring)

Italian ceramic tiles inspired this cushioned sheet vinyl flooring with a slight embossing on the surface. A moisture-resistant backing permits installation on any grade level, including basements. Note how continuation of pattern unifies both areas. (Italian Classic by Armstrong)

The authentic reproduction of hand-crafted tiles in a cushioned vinyl flooring fools the eye, but is softer underfoot. (Colonial Paver by Armstrong)

would be safest. In such applications, skid-proof surfacing might top the priority list, although not as important in an area designed for adult use.

Soil-hiding properties are built into many of the most elegant resilient flooring patterns. Do take time to consider whether the pattern of your choice will disguise soil, or will require extra attention. For instance, large black-and-white squares, so often chosen, gives you the worst of both extremes. The black shows light soil, while the white highlights anything darker than pale sand.

While the new vinyl floor coverings offer the least amount of maintenance, they still require a little care. Protect them from grinding sand with entrance mats, vacuum and/or sweep them occasionally, and make sure large surface casters and plastic cups protect the flooring from dents.

Measuring

In measuring and making a layout, being accurate pays off. Sheet goods come in rolls which can be applied across the room, or lengthwise, and even on the diagonal for unusual effects. The standard roll

widths are 6, 9, and 12 feet, which is the dimension that must be fitted to your available space. Check first to see if the pattern you are using can be matched when the direction is reversed, or whether you must have the pattern all going in one direction. Then, adjust for matching the pattern in estimating the yardage you require.

Use your floor plan to indicate the direction of the flooring, as a rough guide throughout the installation. In addition to any extra needed for seam matching, include an overage of 3 inches extra all around the room to adjust for any variances in wall plumb.

Extra scraps are wonderful for decorative as well as practical details. Use them under heavy furniture to unobtrusively protect the floor. More inventive applications include covering the tops of coffee tables or cubes, extending the floor pattern up to a window seat, or covering the front or top of a bar.

Application Steps

Installation can involve no more than just laying the sheet in place and cutting it to size, for some types. However, the conventional means of anchoring the flooring includes applying adhesive either over the entire underneath surface, or just around the perimeter. Manufacturers often offer the exact adhesive with instructions for their own products, designed for the best bond.

Here are some general steps for most installations (suggested by Congoleum).

1. Tools: a straight blade utility knife with a good strong blade, not a thin razor; tape measure; carpenter's square or metal yard stick; push broom; shears or heavy scissors; hammer; small ply bar for removing moldings.

2. Prepare floors by removing everything not stationary. Then, remove floor moldings carefully, for reuse later, or for replacement with new cove molding or quarter rounds. Next clean, dry and remove all wax or other foreign materials from the floor. Drive protruding nails flush and renail loose spots. Fill cracks in the subfloor with a hard-setting, non-shrinking patching compound. In effect, you render the underneath surface as flat and smooth as possible. On concrete subfloors, vacuum thoroughly so that the floor is free of all dust.

3. To cut the sheet, find a room larger than the one in which it will finally be used (perhaps the garage?). For intricate cutouts, such as those around pipes, make a paper pattern first, and then copy this onto the surface of the flooring with a non-

marking crayon, such as a china marker. Maintain your 3-inch extra margin in making your cutouts; you can finalize them on the spot for an exact fit within the room.

4. Once marking and cutting are completed, roll up the flooring with surface in, so that the roll's length is parallel to the room's long dimension.

5. The room should be warm for best results. Subfloor, flooring material and room temperature should be at least 70 degrees F. Allow time for this temperature to be reached.

6. Loosely unroll the flooring, and allow the material to curl up along the room edges. Adjust so that the pattern is running true, and that the edges are about equally lapped up the wall.

Excess material is cut away with a utility knife and a carpenter's square or straightedge to fit the sheet.

Available in 12-foot and 6-foot widths, Armstrong's Tredway cushioned flooring is easily moved into position and can cover most rooms without seams. Material can be laid over existing vinyl floor, over plywood particle board, concrete, and most other floors.

7. For outside corners, make a relief cut in the flooring from the top of the lapped up material to where the floor and wall meet.

8. For inside corners, gradually cut down the flooring material until it fits into the corner.

9. Trimming down along the straight sides of the room can be handled in one of two ways. The one which works best for you will depend upon the pliability of the material you have chosen.

(a) Using a sharp straight-bladed utility knife, gradually trim down the flooring material lapped up the wall until it lays flat.

(b) Press the flooring into the right angle where floor and wall meet, using your fingers or a piece of 2" x 4". Then, lay a metal yardstick or your carpenter's square as close to the wall as possible, and cut along this with a sharp utility knife. Put the yardstick flat on the floor, so that you are cutting the edge that is on the wall.

(c) The maximum allowable gap between the wall or baseboard should be about ⅛ inch less than the thickness of the molding that is to be reapplied after the flooring is installed. Flooring goes flush to the door frames.

10. Once the floor covering has been fitted, you can adhere it to the subfloor. Roll about ½ of the material face in, or lay it back upon itself.

11. To adhere the flooring completely, apply adhesive to the subfloor. One of the most convenient systems uses a foam adhesive. You just spray bands around the perimeter of the subfloor, and about 12 inches apart running the length of the room. Roll the flooring material immediately back into the wet adhesive. Take the push broom and completely flatten the flooring material onto the wet adhesive, being certain that all air pockets are expelled. Repeat the process identically on the second half of the room.

Staples or cement are used to fasten sheet at edges. Cement is necessary in places a staple gun cannot reach, where no molding will hide staples, or when staples cannot penetrate subfloor such as concrete. Note five-bead adhesive applicator.

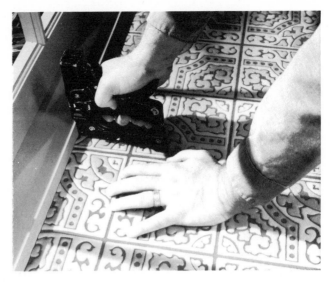

Some flooring can be installed with staples only. Space them at 3-inch intervals directly into flooring that will take heavy-duty staples, along edges that can be covered with molding.

12. To adhere the flooring at the perimeter only, the procedure is even simpler. This is suitable over concrete subfloors and well-bonded flooring materials. You will want to prepare old floor covering that is to remain underneath by applying a strong solution of dishwasher detergent about 8 inches from the wall around the room, and around any protrusions such as columns that will be bordered by the flooring. Let the solution stand until you can remove all traces of old wax and dirt, and allow to dry thoroughly.

Then, fit and cut the flooring, lay it back for ½ of the room and apply adhesive around the perimeter and around any columns, pipes or other protrusions, about one inch in from where the edge of the flooring will be. Re-position the flooring on the adhesive, go over it with a push broom to eliminate air pockets, and proceed to lay the rest of the material.

13. Finishing includes putting back the quarter rounds and other moldings. While you are at it, you might consider some of the new cove-moldings that are designed to go with resilient flooring. These come in 4-foot lengths, and are easily applied with adhesive for a modern-looking treatment. You can buy pre-made outer corner sections, and can then miter inner corners for a custom look. Finish doorways with metal trim.

14. Installation without adhesive is possible with some of the cushioned flooring. The fitting is hand-

Finished job looks professional when flooring is carefully applied. Tredway even has a built-in resilience that allows adjustment if slightly undercut or too loose. It both stretches and contracts to make up for slight errors. (All photos from Armstrong Cork Co.)

85

led the same way as for other flooring, but the final fit should not be closer to the walls or baseboard trim than ⅛ inch. This allows the flooring to relax and give a bit, if need be. For the same reason, raise moldings or quarter rounds slightly from the flooring material and nail them into the baseboard, not the floor. Metal trims at doorways should not be fastened through the flooring material either.

Coping with seams. A necessary evil for broken-up space, or large areas, but take heart! Sometimes it is easier to fit two separate pieces than to be exact with one piece. Here is a system for putting down invisible seams.

1. Fit the first sheet to the room. Apply adhesive in a strip to within 8 inches of the seam area, and flatten the sheet against the subfloor with a push broom.

2. Overlap the second sheet at the seam so the design unit matches across the sheets. Make sure that the design matches EXACTLY.

3. After matching the design, leave the overlap and fit the second sheet to the room. Apply adhesive to within 8 inches of the seam area, and flatten the sheet against the subfloor with a push broom.

4. Place a steel straightedge on top of the two overlapping pieces where the seam will be, generally an inch or so in from the top edge of the overlap. Cut straight down through both layers of the flooring material with a very sharp straight blade utility knife.

5. Turn back both pieces, and remove the extra flooring that has been trimmed off. The result will be an exact seam, since both sides of it were created with a single cut. The final step is to apply a band of adhesive 3 inches in from the edge of the sheets, and then press both sides of the seam completely flat to the subfloor. Clean off any excess adhesive with whatever is recommended, and make sure both sides are flat.

6. A seam-sealing agent is used to fill in the seam, and keep it free from dirt collection in the future. Special applicators, and material applied with a slotted nozzle, make this finishing easy. Do not omit to finish and seal the seam before dirt creeps into the crevice.

Many tiles are made to give a continuous patterned feeling to a room. ("Lisboa" vinyl tiles by Goodyear)

Tiles

Many do-it-yourselfers consider resilient flooring tiles the easiest method to assure a good-looking floor, because you only have to cope with a limited amount of flooring at a time. Some of the other advantages of resilient tiles, which come in different patterns and colors, are:

• They are often the most economical choices when dealing with an area with many cut-up small spaces.

• You can create your own decorative effects by altering the tiles to suit your own design motifs.

• They are easier to correct than sheet goods, if you make a mistake.

• Some designs are made so that seams are invisibly worked into the overall pattern; others can be applied so closely that seams virtually disappear.

Tools

You will need a good straightedge or carpenter's square, heavy-duty cutting knife or shears, notched trowel for adhesive if you are using it, 6-foot ruler or heavy tape measure for marking center lines, and chalked line or heavy grease pencil for marking center lines.

Installation

Measure and make a layout. This is done most easily with graph paper, and is the place to start, especially if using contrasting tiles. Among the possibilities is use of "feature strips", offered by some companies. These come in the same thickness as the field tiles, in ¼, ½, 1 and 2 inch widths. Strips are generally two feet in length and in solid colors.

Here are some of the more popular tile flooring patterns. However, you can develop your own personalized designs by cutting out freeform shapes, or making variations on the usual geometric arrangements.

- Arrange four tiles in a square, and separate them with strips for a large tattersal plaid effect.

- Use strips to set off one area that needs special emphasis, such as the floor extending two feet in front of a bar or fireplace. You could even use a different color for this smaller area.

- Simulate a contrasting color "rug" for part of the flooring by using a separate color and bordering it with strips.

- Use the simple, classic checkerboard alternation of two different colors of square tiles.

- Create a herringbone effect by placing two matched tiles side by side, alternating them with two contrasting tiles. Alternate the next row color for color, in sets of twos.

- Create large squares in a vast space by making checkerboard blocks of four tiles each of the same color.

- Surround one tile with eight tiles of a different color in a square, then reverse the combination for the next section.

- Consider using half-tiles cut on the diagonal for an infinite variety of patterns based on patchwork quilt designs.

- Consider laying all of your tiles diagonally.

Prepare subfloor. Follow same steps as for sheet tile. Make sure nails are flush, fill in obvious dents, and generally make as flat a surface as possible. Prepare a good clean wax-free surface, so that the adhesive will stick properly. Check to see whether a special subflooring is needed, especially in protecting the tiles from dampness. Tiles tend to separate when exposed to water leakage.

Mark the center lines both lengthwise and across the width of the room to use as a guide in laying the tiles. This can be done by chalking a plumb line, stretching it across the room, and snapping it to make chalk beneath it. Allow the adhesive materials to sit in the room at a temperature of over 70 degrees to help facilitate the sticking. Remove quarter rounds at the perimeter for re-use later (or add new moldings later).

Adhering the tiles. Simple, with the new self-stick types. For a more durable installation, use tiles that require adhesive applied to the floor. In either case, the progression of laying the tiles is the same.

Planning the exact placement of your tiles. This will depend upon the sides of the room, although you start from the center. The important point is to leave enough space on all margins of the room to fit a large-enough sized tile. Anything less than one quarter of a tile is going to be difficult to fit, and will not look very good, either.

The standard method of laying out tiles is to bisect the room lengthwise, and then crosswise. You start with the tiles in one quarter of the room, starting from the center.

Here's where you adjust your measurements to have relatively equal amounts of tile at each border. You can line the tiles up so that the edge of the tile is right on the cross-secting lines in the center of the room. In this case, dead center is framed by the corners and side seams of the four center tiles. Or, another system calls for centering one tile on the line in the center of the room. You can either center or start on the line in either direction to achieve the adequate border-size pieces you need.

Depending upon the width of the room, your best plan may be to center the tiles across the bisecting line, or, depending on the length of the room, you may need to begin by laying the tiles on the line lengthwise.

To lay tiles diagonally, start by stretching and marking a line from one corner at a 45° angle to the other wall. Center the tiles along this line, or place them to one side of it.

Lay the tiles. Do one-quarter of the room at a time, starting with the center corner, and laying one row lengthwise and one widthwise. If you are using separate adhesive, spread it with a notched trowel, one section at a time. You will want enough to create a good bond, but not so much that it will ooze out between the tiles under pressure. Wait until the adhesive develops some tackiness to the touch, without grabbing completely. Press tiles into position without scooping the adhesive.

Begin filling in the rows adjacent to those marked off in the center, and complete the first quarter with all

1. These are the steps in laying tiles, carpet squares, or wood blocks. To locate the center of the room, find the center of each wall, then pull a chalked string taut to the opposite wall and snap a straight line on the subfloor. This allows the room to be "squared off" so tile is laid parallel to the walls.

3. Adhesive should be thinly brushed, troweled, or rolled on, so that when tile is laid, adhesive will not push up between tiles or cause them to slip underfoot. Self-stick tiles do not need adhesive.

2. Lay a row of loose tiles along the chalkline from the center point to one side wall and one end wall. Measure distance between wall and the last full tile. If this space is less than a half-tile, snap a new chalkline and move half a width of tile closer to the opposite wall. Check right angles. Now, do the same with the other row. This will improve the appearance of the floor and eliminate the need for fitting small pieces of tile next to the walls.

4. Place tiles carefully so that you do not scoop up any adhesive that is beneath them. Set them into position working from the guidelines established at the center of the room, working toward the corner.

5. One-quarter section of the room is laid at a time, with each tile set firmly and tightly to adjoining tile, so there are no visible joints.

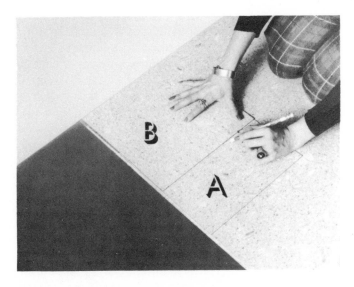

6. To cut and fit the tiles next to the wall, place a loose tile (A) squarely on top of the last full tile closest to the wall. On top of this, place another tile (B) and slide it until it butts against the wall. Using the edge of the top tile (B) as a guide, mark the tile under it with a pencil. With a pair of shears, cut tile (A) along the pencil line. It will fit into space near the wall.

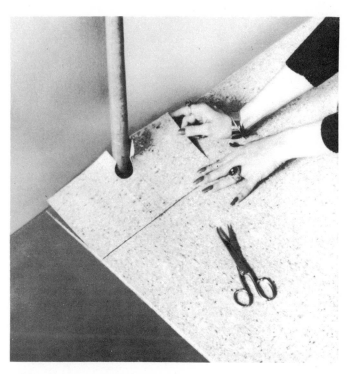

To fit around pipes, etc., make a paper pattern to fit the space exactly. Then trace the outline onto the tile and cut with shears. Insert tile into border space with rough edge against the wall. (Azrock photos)

full tiles. Then, go on and repeat the procedure in the second, third, and fourth quarters. Go over the tile with something heavy to make sure the edges are firmly flattened.

Finishing around the room's edges. This calls for cutting the tiles. You need a bit of give in the fit, so make them about ⅛ inch shy of the wall, which will be covered by coves or moldings.

To cut border tiles to fit, place them next to the wall so that they overlap the full tiles already installed. Then draw a line across the tile to be cut, where the overlap takes place. With a sharp blade and steel straightedge, or sharp scissors, cut off the extra tile that overlaps, and the new fitted tile is ready for installation. Complete all tiles on one side of the room, apply adhesive, and set them in place. Then do other edges.

To cut out tiles to go around moldings or pipes, make a paper pattern first. Then, use the pattern to cover the tile and to guide your cutting lines with scissors. For difficult measuring and pattern-making jobs, you might want to invest in a contour gauge. Otherwise, use the trial-and-error method on a paper pattern first, and then commit the pattern to the tile. Remember to always be sure that the pattern is right side up and the tile right side up, so that your cutouts aren't reversed.

A good job will appear seamless except where you want the seams to show. Here, a pattern is created with vinyl asbestos feature strips, for a totally custom look. The overall tile pattern is "Kingston" in Azrock vinyl asbestos floor tile.

Entrance areas are particularly suited for floor tile treatments. Here a classic checkerboard of black and white tiles proves dramatic. (Azrock vinyl asbestos floor tile)

Prefinished Wood Flooring

Once the answer for someone who simply didn't want to be bothered with finishing, wood floors today are fashionable and practical, if one of the more adventurous approaches is used.

The biggest news in the wood flooring area is the relatively recent development of laminated wood blocks with prefinished surfaces, and planks that are prefinished for the do-it-yourselfer. Installation systems have been developed that make use of these materials in basements practical, even though they are below grade or on grade. As with other flooring, you need to check whatever wood flooring you choose to make sure that it is the right kind to use in your particular situation: directly on concrete, on subflooring, or whether a special kind of subfloor situation is demanded.

One necessary word of caution about wood floors (or any kind of quality flooring, for that matter), is that you will have unending trouble if your basement floods. These products are designed to be used with the protection of a vapor barrier or some other device. But, take a good look at the area in terms of its susceptibility to flooding before investing in any flooring that might be damaged. And, consult with a contractor to take care of this major problem if it exists, before installing anything that could be ruined.

There are many reasons for choosing wood flooring. With a good finish it offers many of the easy-care properties of resilient tiles. Or, a naturalist may simply prefer the delightful counterplay of grains, textural illusions, and pattern possibilities available in using differently stained wood flooring sections. Then a traditionalist might be slightly uncomfortable with the obviously untraditional use of resilient flooring or wall-to-wall carpeting with period pieces, such as those found in Early American rooms. Or, you may want to use natural wood flooring as a foil to your accent rugs.

Decorative choices will lead you to both light and dark finishes of a variety of woods, although oak is the admitted leader. The blocks range from rather formal finished looks to casual, plank and distressed wood effects, and the classic parquet patterns.

For really rustic country looks, some planks come with factory-installed pegs (sometimes in walnut for contrast) at the strip ends to simulate the real pegging of old authentic plank floors. These are often provided in packages of random lengths, and widths of 3 to 7 inches, all the better in simulating the real thing. Sometimes the edges are even beveled to look like the large cracks in the floorboards that abound in museum restorations. Adhesive application of these planks would make our forefathers green with envy; it eliminates potential squeaks and creaks of plank flooring.

Bruce Village Plank in oak can be laid in mastic over concrete or nailed to other floors. Widths are 3", 5", and 7", with random lengths and ⅓" thickness. Finished in either smooth texture, or wire-brushed surface for an antiqued appearance, with pegs or without. (Bruce Hardwood Floors)

Bruce Ranch Plank is laid in alternating 2¼" and 3¼" widths with factory installed genuine walnut pegs. Edges are beveled to accentuate the plank appearance of alternating widths, and surface is factory finished. (Bruce Hardwood Flooring Products)

Cumberland Oak Parquet blocks are 6" square; they are installed in adhesive over almost any subfloor, including, concrete with a tongue and groove. Various finishes are available. (Bruce Hardwood Floors)

Tough prefinished teak is the world's strongest wood and a good choice for family rooms, especially since it is moisture resistant. Four 6" x 6" squares are bound into 12" by 12" blocks by a cotton mesh backing to give this pattern fast installation. (Bruck Hardwood Floors)

Installation

Preparing the subfloor. As important a step in installing block prefinished wood flooring as for any other flooring, just follow the manufacturer's recommendations for cleaning concrete slabs so they are ready to accept the flooring. This includes leveling out and filling in any crevices that would create an uneven finished surface, and preparing the surface to assure a good bond.

Old wood floors may be all the underneath surface you need. In this case, make sure that all nails are flush or countersunk. If the surface is in really bad shape, consider laying a new subfloor that will give you the necessary evenness. This is particularly important for self-stick and thinner block flooring.

If the old wood floor will do, then rough-sand it to remove all traces of wax or finish that would impede the adhesion of the new blocks. You can rent the sanding equipment from local companies, or have a local company do this sanding job for you. Take care that dust and dirt created during this preparation process are not allowed to hurt the new prefinished flooring blocks.

At this stage remove any moldings or quarter-rounds for replacement once the job is completed. The flooring itself will add anywhere up to an inch of height once installed, so the quarter rounds will be correspondingly higher. Also consider changing the moldings if they will not suit the new look of the floor. And, order any nosing strips that you might need to adjust the height differences in the doorways from one room to another. Some block manufacturers provide them factory-finished to match the blocks themselves, for a complete and custom look.

Any special application step, such as the addition of a vapor barrier, takes place at this stage as well. Make sure that you can quickly go on to the further steps once you begin floor preparation, so that anything that is perishable will be safely covered within the shortest time possible.

Installing prefinished flooring is most successful when you follow the directions of the manufacturers exactly, in terms of choice of adhesive and suitability to the area. Here are some general tips for doing the job easily and professionally. For more hints, read the section on resilient tiles.

1. Make a layout, including any free-standing pipes or protrusions that will figure in your overall scheme. Allow about 5 percent in additional planks or tiles.

2. For plank layouts, try to vary the plank end placements, so that no two ends in adjacent rows are in line. Vary widths of the planks as well, to recreate the casual flooring of our forefathers.

3. Review the ideas for alternating tiles in the resilient tile section for effectively creating a block wood floor pattern. Mark your plan carefully on graph paper to scale. You can use the same patterns to alternate wood grain direction or wood tone for subtle effects. The layout also serves as a guide in ordering the number of blocks needed in each wood tone.

4. Allow your wood to rest in the room for a few days before installing it, to make sure that it is warm, dry, and compatible.

5. Use a chalked plumb line to mark the center area of the room for installing the flooring, as is done with tiles. Use the most attractive pieces for the center of the room, and save the less attractive pieces for perimeters. Since there is a natural variance in real wood, your preference to tight grains, loose grains, etc., is the deciding factor in choosing the keystone tiles to start the center display.

6. If installing with mastic, be careful that you place the block rather than scooping it into position. Then, take advantage of the tongue and groove edging to make sure that the blocks are securely anchored one to another.

7. Apply the adhesive and install the blocks one section at a time, checking your work as you go.

8. With most blocks, you can fit exactly to wall surfaces. Use the instructions for laying tile to cut out and around for exact fits. Finish by replacing the moldings or quarter rounds by nailing them to the wall, not to the flooring.

9. Keep the flooring clean and it will give you years of wear.

Existing Wood Floors

Refinishing old wood flooring can be one of the easiest and least expensive methods of giving a floor a new look. First check to make sure that the flooring is thick enough to withstand sanding to remove all the surface material. Then, carefully patch any areas that are waterstained or otherwise damaged, or it will show up in the refinishing.

A floor sanding machine can be rented from local firms that specialize in such rentals, often the local hardware store. This is a messy job in terms of the dust it creates, but a necessary one to get down to the wood surface so it will be as handsome as when new.

If floor refinishing is not your cup of tea, then by all means enlist the aid of a professional floor finisher. Discuss with him the kinds of stain and finish you hope to achieve, and leave either the entire job in his hands, or arrange with him to handle the finishing yourself, once he has done the sanding.

The most important element in successful floor refinishing is to have a realistic, good plan for timing each stage of the job. Once the floor has been sanded, you must press on to the sealing, staining, and finishing stages or risk ruining the entire project by allowing dirt to become embedded in the fresh, virgin surface.

For sanding, make sure you have ample sanding materials so that if they become soiled, you can continue with replacements. On a relatively new floor, the surface may be removed with little or no trouble, but an old floor may require extra time for sanding away countless years of wax buildup, which makes the job go slower. And, you'll save time in the long run by following the sanding rental company's suggestions for using their equipment and preparing the room for a quick completion of this stage of the job.

Add to the amount of time specified on your floor stain or finishing material to be on the safe side. The manufacturer is giving guides of set-up time, which might be longer in your case. A sudden turn to damp cold weather will impede the drying of the floor, both for the first coat and for proper set-up before the second coat can be applied. Just as a watched pot does not boil, a floor in the process of being finished simply does not hurry, especially if you do not allow enough time to adequately complete the job.

The New Finish

Choose a new floor finish that will stand the test of time in your family room. Any extreme application, such as bleached-wood looks or very dark staining, should be scrutinized for a while, to make sure that you will want to keep that look for as long as the floor will last. On the other hand, select a floor finish that will make a positive statement in the room. There's no sense in going to all that trouble unless you are creating something you feel is really beautiful.

Stains can darken woods, warm them up, cool the tones down, and bring the color of the flooring into better relationship with whatever paneling you might plan for the room. Another consideration in choosing a stain or color for your flooring is the tone of any wood furniture that will be placed upon it. You will want a family feeling, but a pleasing contrast with the other wood tones and the flooring.

Pleasingly bare floors have been with us long enough so that they are no longer new. This look is ideally suited to rooms that are decorated with wicker, bamboo, butcherblock, or any of the light, white modern furniture pieces. You need to start with pretty good flooring in this decorative treatment, since every inch of the wood and its grain will show through.

The finishes available for floors today are almost impervious to wear, spotting, and normal rough and tumbling. Among these are the acrylics and polyurethanes that look like older conventional floor finishes, but wear like iron. In this area, you can choose the degree of gloss you want, from a bowling alley high-gloss finish to the subtler semi-glosses that have the elegance and restraint of old-fashioned waxed floors. Usually, the high glosses are most durable, but

Machines are essential for floor refinishing, and can often be rented. A large drum-type sanding machine with vacuum attachment is best for main floor area, while a power edger does sides, as shown.

Hand scraping is sometimes needed at edges and in corners even with an edger-sander. Be careful with all sanding not to gouge, and go over the job enough times to create a good surface, sanding with the grain.

look for the right compromise between the look you want and the wear resistance you need.

Stages in floor finishing include sanding, and thorough vacuuming to remove all dust. Then, clean the sanded floor with a dry absorbent mop. Open-grained wood floors need not be filled unless an ultra-smooth finish is desired. The slight bit of texture that results from the natural graining adds to the overall effect of some flooring. However, with others, you will want to apply a filler. This is a varnish or vegetable oil containing a silicate. It blocks the porosity of the open-pore wood and prevents lifting the fibers in the wood. Fillers are somewhat creamy in texture, or paste-like. Brush them on and wipe off the excess across the grain of the wood, leaving pores filled and ready for varnish, stain, or paint. Check the manufacturer's instructions to see when stain should be applied in conjunction with a filler, to be sure that the filler will work with the sealant you have chosen.

After staining, finish with a sealing agent. One popular choice is a low-lustre clear varnish applied in one or two coats. The important thing is to protect the wood surface by creating a sturdy barrier between it and any dirt. Wax alone cannot do this. Brush the varnish on liberally, going with the grain, then stroke across the grain. This way, a completely flat surface will be flowing in and over the wood. Take a small area at a time, and go to the next area rapidly, before any edges have set up. Start your brush in the dry unvarnished area, and stroke into the wet area. Use a very fine grit of sandpaper to go over the first coat lightly once it is completely dry. Then, finish with a second coat applied the same way.

Another approach is to use a clear wood seal or a penetrating finish, and then wax can be applied for added protection. Follow the instructions of the manufacturer, who will probably suggest applying freely with a lamb's wool pad, cloth or brush. Work fast in removing excess, since penetration takes about 20 minutes for some products. A uniform application is important to give good protection. If you spot variations, wipe off the excess anyway, then apply a second coat after the first is completely dry.

Stencils

Stenciling is one highly effective means of adding surface decoration to floors you are refinishing. By using them on the wood grain background, you can achieve both pattern and the look of a natural surface. Techniques are covered in the next section on painted floors. One difference in using stencils on natural floors is that you will want to make sure that the paint or stain you use for the pattern will not "bleed" into raw wood. Follow the manufacturer's directions for

priming the floor to take the stencil. In some cases, the stencil pattern can be applied between coats of finish.

Use a tough piece of cardboard to make a stencil for each of the colors you plan to use, and cut out the appropriate shapes for each. For instance, your large background color might be a tree-shaped wedge in white, repeated around a circle, with a border band to delineate a square. Tape stencil in place. Dab paint through stencil opening until paint density desired is achieved. Repeat with second section, or alternate sections if you might smudge the design already down.

Wait until you are absolutely sure the first stencil color is dry before applying the smaller, second color. Use the guidelines sketched or taped to the floor to line up the second stencil, in this case, a gold color in pie-wedge shapes over the white tree shapes, and an open circle around the central motif.

The handsome results are well worth the time and effort to personalize a floor. You can stencil over painted surfaces as well as regular flooring, as long as the base surface is clean and assures a good paint bond. Protect your handiwork with several coats of clear polyurethane finish. (Pictures from 1001 Decorating Ideas Magazine)

Stenciled floors are wonderful accompaniments to gaily colored countrified family rooms, especially those with a Pennsylvania Dutch theme, since they are softer and subtler than painted floor treatments.

Painting Floors

Painting floors is the traditional means of covering existing flooring inexpensively. It has taken on a new importance with the development of stencils and other patterns for highly creative treatments.

Painted wood floors invariably retain some of the outlines of the strips, blocks, or planks of the wood themselves. You can decide to subdue this by creating a covering pattern that disguises it, or by choosing a medium to dark tone that visually tones down the natural lines. Or, you can capitalize on the floor's pattern by using light colors that allow it to come through or patterns that emphasize these built-in lines. For instance, you can create a stencil pattern that exactly fits within the margins of the parquet squares of a floor. Another technique is to mask off each successive strip of flooring and color it a different color for a striped flooring effect. The possibilities are endless.

Preparation for a well-done painted wood floor is pretty much the same as for refinishing the floor. You must remove all wax and dirt, and in some cases sand down through the old finish if it will not enable a good bond. If the floor has already been painted, follow the standard procedures for repainting surfaces. Make sure the old paint is clean and wax free, and that the new paint is compatible enough to adhere well to it. Remove chipped paint and sand those areas smooth before adding a new coat.

Choose a paint designed to withstand the rigors of constant abuse, because an application on the floor is just about as strenuous in wear as any application you will ever make. Old-timers will recommend deck paint, along with some of the newer compositions that are tougher today. The qualities you should determine are the paint's ability to cover, its suitability over the surface you are working with, and its durability. The set-up time is also important, as is the time between coats and amount of time before the room can be safely used.

The basic color should not highlight every slightly dirty footmark, so keep it in the middle range. In addition to that, consider the overall effect of the color on the other furnishings in the room, and its relationship to the wall decoration (especially paneling).

Take the time to cover part of the floor area as a test, if you are at all unsure about the color you have chosen. Pure paint colors act entirely differently in daylight and nighttime lighting, and you will want to see the actual paint in both situations. For instance, you may find that a yellow is perfect for the slightly diffused lighting it would get on the walls. However, in a shiny enamel, it is far too intense when brought to life by direct sunlight streaming across a painted floor. Or, the periwinkle blue that looked soft and lively in a store might be dull and dreary in a basement room with little available lighting at all. For the final paint job, mix all the paint at once so you will not have color changes.

How often have you heard the one about not painting yourself into a corner? Without a good layout plan, it is an error just waiting to be made. Let forewarned be forearmed.

The materials you will need for painting can be as simple as a wide brush for the main area, edging brush for borders, paint bucket, drop cloths and rags for mop-ups, and a piece of cardboard to help prevent getting the paint on the molding. However, there are many painting accessories to make this job faster and easier, with an ingenious switch of application. For instance, a roller with handle designed for a ceiling paint job can save your back while doing the floor. And there are sponge-like "brushes" that offer good covering and easy edging.

Painted wood floors may take longer to dry than you think, since the paint between the cracks will tend to puddle. Be absolutely sure to wait until this paint is dry before recoating or considering the job done. Close off the area between coats and while the final coat is drying, since a painted floor is one giant dust-catcher. And when in doubt, leave the furniture out another day while the paint dries completely.

Stenciling painted floors. Stenciling can add pattern after the floor has been given a good solid color treatment. Traditional stencils are most suitable for

Early American rooms of a casual nature. The early stenciled floors were country folk's ways of simulating the rugs that they either could not afford, or could not get in the new land.

One good source for designs are the many books of folk painting motifs. You can scale these up to make all-over patterns, simulate rug patterns with repeated borders, or merely add interest to the border of a painted floor. In fact, you can even buy reproduction templates of the old traditional patterns in book form, ready for use in decorating your own floor.

One good idea in using stencils is to make a number of templates, so that you can continue decorating the floor by rotating them. This lessens the chance of the template itself becoming over-saturated with wet paint.

You can use the lines of the wood floor as a guide in laying your stencils. Then, masking tape to hold them in place will help avoid smearing. This delicate job is handled best with good brushes suitable to the paint you are using for decoration (usually acrylic) and "easy does it" is the slogan for this operation. To avoid going under the edges of the stencil, dab the paint on, moving the brush up and down, instead of using horizontal brush strokes. Be careful in removing the stencil once the paint is applied, to prevent smearing the job.

It is a good idea to try applying new stencils to another surface before committing yourself to the floor, so that you are comfortable and proficient at it. Then, start with an area of the room that commands the least attention.

Multiple-colored effects are created through the use of coordinated stencils, one for each color, much like the silk screening of fabric. You use the same key guidelines for the stencils in each color, so that each successive color is properly placed in relationship to the previous colors. It goes without saying that you must wait until each color dries before applying the next one.

Stencil patterns need not be limited to traditional designs. Many of the most popular contemporary geometric patterns would be easily adapted to stencil application. For example, you might develop a repeat pattern that includes a box with a smaller circle in it, for a lively geometric effect that is simple but effective.

Splattering. Here is another painted floor technique that spans the gap from old to new. Good for uneven flooring you want to disguise, or where you want an interesting floor treatment but no directional pattern. The effect depends upon the amount of splatter and the colors you choose for it. With many colors, your floor will be as colorful as a Jackson Pollock painting. Subtler approaches confine the colors to one hue or perhaps two. An example would be a medium blue floor with splatters of white, light blue, royal blue, and surprise touches of red.

It is a good idea to start by covering the walls near the floor with paper, so that no splatters land on the wrong areas. Then, dip an ample, stiff brush in the paint pail of the splatter color, and tap the brush across a stick, so that drops and droplets spray from it. Try this a few times on an old drop cloth, so that you can regulate the direction and the amount of paint that drops each time. Allow drying time before applying each new color. The end result is both casual and colorful. And you will have one of the most personal floor coverings in town.

Large custom effects. These designs can be totally free-form, or achieved through the assist of straight edges and compass arcs. Once again, graph paper comes to the rescue in plotting a pretty pattern or picture to apply to the floor. While you are at it, consider the placement of the furniture so that your decoration will have the greatest impact.

Your imagination is the only limit in choosing a floor pattern. You might take a cue from a wallcovering, and pick up one of the motifs for repetition in the same scale, or a different one, on the floor. For instance, a pattern with daisies can be duplicated in the painted floor with gigantic, stylized versions of the same flower. Or, an overscaled geometric flooring might accent a geometric upholstery fabric. Or, you might want to accent the sweep of circular seating by outlining it on the floor in paint.

A lathing strip or simple string becomes a supersized compass with the addition of a pencil at one end and a tack to anchor it on the other. Once you have painted the basic color on the floor, use such simple devices to make sure that your pattern is applied with sharpness. Unless your painting hand is incredibly steady, go over the outer edge of the area to be painted in outline with masking tape. Paint around, near this border, and fill in the center. Remove the masking tape while the paint is still wet so that the edge lines will have a chance to smooth out.

A repeated pattern that is too large for convenient stenciling can be traced onto the floor with cutout shapes. For instance, if you have chosen 2-foot daisies, you can make a cardboard pattern of a petal and trace it to mark the positioning of each petal around the center. It will save time if you can standardize your applications rather than by doing all of them freehand.

For all decorated painted floors it is a good idea to protect your artwork with a coat or two of clear polyurethane. Check in advance that the paints you are using will be compatible with a top coat of clear material. This protection will enhance the patterns, preserve your work, and smooth the surfaces between the base coat and decorative paint.

Concrete slab floors. The only paint these floors take well is the kind that seals them, such as a latex floor enamel. This is one of the least costly means of covering the floor, but it is also one that may be troublesome in the long run. Any moisture remaining in the uncured concrete can cause chipping and peeling. If you use the previously described techniques for stenciling and decorating wooden floors on concrete, you can elevate a simple paint job above the usual "basement" look.

In most cases, a painted concrete floor will need special preparation, such as rough sanding, before another material can be used over it. If you are considering this as a temporary measure and plan to add another covering in the future, you might be better off forging ahead with the floor covering of your choice from the start. In any case, make sure that you choose the proper paint, and that it can be covered later with little effort.

7. Personality Walls

Family or recreation room walls should be decorative and sturdy. Luckily, both are easy to achieve with the myriad of materials available for wall coverings today. Paint is the least expensive, while wall coverings and paneling are popular choices, and are often the most resistant to damage. Or you can apply fabric for a total wall treatment.

Any of these materials can be used in almost any room, with some preparation. All are within the easy reach of the do-it-yourselfer.

Paint

Painted walls are the least costly; however, quality counts when it comes to choosing paint. So does matching the paint to its use. Generally, water-based paints in a matte finish are best, since they give off no fumes, are easy to clean up if spills occur, and are available in many colors. Tell your paint dealer the rough amount of surface to be covered, and get all the paint you need at once, to be sure it is exactly matched.

Matte finishes are favorites for most solid wall surfaces; semi-glosses and even high glosses are effectively used for woodwork. These smoother-surfaced paints are effective in areas that are prone to handmarks or a buildup of grease that will need washing. They are often used in kitchen and bath areas for just this reason.

Stucco and textured paints are options for badly damaged walls. They also can cover unwanted textures such as those of concrete block. However, they are difficult to repaint, so be sure that you want to keep that texture before committing it to the wall.

Do-it-yourself graphics incorporate these problem high strip windows, so often found in basements. Paneling strips and paint are combined for the geometric wall treatment, taken from the colors of the carpet used throughout the room. (Ludlow "Barclay Tartan" carpet of Anso Nylon, from Allied Chemical)

Stuccoed Mediterranean effect covers the walls and ceilings in this handsome room. Z-Ment Stucco applies directly to existing walls and ceilings, comes premixed, and needs no water. (Z-Ment Stucco photo)

Different textures of applicators and thicknesses of stucco used determine the final wall textures with this material. A strong brush gives one effect, while trowel application gives a less directional, overall pattern. (Z-Ment Stucco photo)

If texture is your cup of tea, experiment with the various effects that you can achieve through the use of it. Using a heavily bristled brush, you can make swirls, herringbone effects, or cross-hatch patterns in the wet textured paint. Highly textured paints such as stucco (which acts somewhat like molten plaster), can be raised in points, flattened with abstract-like daubing, or even deeply grooved with the use of notched trowels. But just because these materials are thicker than conventional paint, do not assume that they will solve a leaking wall problem. You must treat walls that show moisture or leakage with wall sealer before any paint will successfully adhere to them.

Special graphic effects can also be created through the use of flat paints. Some of the techniques for painting floors, such as stenciling and using large straight edges and compasses, are equally applicable to walls. Consider setting off a special area, such as that behind a bar, in a different color. And you might even add to the effect by creating a painted border of yet another color or treatment.

To create a supergraphic effect, make a layout of the wall first. Measure and mark on graph paper the exact dimensions of the walls between windows, doors, and add other factors, such as radiators or moldings.

Relate your painted wall design to the placement of the furniture in the room. Do this by making sure

Broad half-circle bands span two walls in navy, poppy, and yellow on a white background to give the super graphic that is all the major decoration a plain room needs. It keys the furniture scheme, as well as the floor. Sofa is actually a Hide-A-Bed. (Simmons Co.)

technique is particularly useful for coordinating joining areas such as staircases.

Painting Techniques

Good painting techniques make the difference between a botched up job and one that is effortless and effective. Start with the proper equipment for the job, which can be purchased at the same time you pick up your paint. For water-based paint (the choice for most do-it-yourselfers), you will probably need the following: roller, roller tray, mixing bucket, sash brush, drop cloths, rags for spills, and ladder. If you plan on painting the ceiling, add a long-handled roller as well. Nylon brushes are best for water-based paints. Then, follow these steps:

1. Prepare the walls. Make sure chips, cracks, and any other surface repairs that need fixing are handled well before you start painting, so that they can be allowed to dry and reworking can be done. You will want to scrape with a paint scraper any areas that are blistered or chipped. Then, sandpaper the edges to feather them so they do not show through the new paint job.

that the lamps, seating units or shelving that you plan to use will not distort or cover up the wall decoration.

Accent walls are often created through the simple technique of changing the paint color on one wall. The accent wall should have a more attention-getting color than the other walls in the room, but should maintain a pleasing relationship to the other wall colors. One way of integrating the accent wall with the rest of the room is to paint all woodwork and molding the same color as the accent wall. Another technique is to use the accent wall color on the lower half of the wall up to a chair-rail molding, topped with the general color used in a room. Since the accent wall colors are usually darker, you have the added bonus of having a lower wall that will show soil less.

Coordinating Colors

Relating two rooms through coordinated paint need not mean a mere repetition of the same color. Choose another tint or shade of the hue for a second room within view of the family room. For instance, with a semi-closed-off workshop, you might use antique gold in the family room, and a lighter, softer gold in the workshop. Another method is to choose an accent color from the main room as the main color in a second room. For instance, you might have a predominantly blue and white scheme in the family room with accents of red. The powder room could be entirely white and red, with accents of blue. The schemes would relate, but without exact duplication. This

A sharp scraper combined with a little muscle will reduce blisters and flaking surfaces almost level on both woodwork and walls. Sandpaper finishes the leveling process to prepare for paint.

Larger cracks call for patching with plaster, then sanding once the patches have dried thoroughly. Small holes and cracks can be repaired with spackling compound, which is smoothed while wet and then sanded when dry. Your electric sander will be a great assist for large repairing jobs, to give walls a smooth surface before applying the new paint.

All repairs need sealing with a primer before they are painted. Allow ample time for drying between each of these steps.

Once you have cleaned out a large hole or crack, patch it with plaster and smooth over the surface with a 4-inch joint finishing knife. Let it dry and sand smooth if you need an even surface.

2. Prepare the woodwork. The two main problems with woodwork are bad surfaces, and possible stainthrough. If the woodwork has previously been varnished or painted, or is flaked, sandpaper it until the gloss and flakes are gone. Check with the dealer for the kind of bonding you will get with the paint you have chosen. In some cases, a special stripper can be used to make woodwork receptive to new paint.

You may need to apply two prime coats of white shellac before woodwork is painted, to keep earlier stains or paint jobs from showing through.

3. Remove hardware, except doorknobs. It usually is easier to replace these than to try not to get paint on them. Cover difficult-to-remove hardware with masking tape.

4. Dust everything. This includes walls, ceilings, and woodwork. If the walls are particularly soiled and greasy, wash them down with detergent. Newly plastered walls need a coat of primer sealer.

All this is to allow the paint job to adhere properly, and is well worth the effort.

5. Protect everything. Floors and furniture that are not intended for painting need protection. Old shower curtains are excellent for drop cloths, and new ones are relatively inexpensive in paint stores. If you use newspaper for the floors, make sure that you use enough thicknesses to prevent leakage. Cover up paneling, too.

The easiest system is to move all furniture to the center of the room, cover it, and work around it. If you have lots of furniture, you may find moving it to one end and then the other easiest.

6. First things first. Start with the ceiling, then do the walls, then do the woodwork. For the broad areas such as ceilings and walls, paint the corners and around the woodwork with a brush, or small edging roller. Then use a broad roller to complete the rest. Work across the width of the ceiling, overlapping a new band of wet paint before the old band dries. Always paint from the dry part into the wet part, to avoid blobs of paint where your roller started. Use the roller in an ''X'' pattern or random pattern, so that no direction shows when the paint dries.

A good even paint job can best be achieved by covering areas about two by three feet at a time, working down from the ceiling.

Start walls at the top, and work across the wall and down from the ceiling. Complete an entire wall before stopping.

Do doors and windows next, and leave them open while they dry. Reposition windows occasionally so that they will not stick in a fixed position. Generally, molding and sashes are done first, then the flatter, broader areas. Finally, do doorways and baseboards. Make the room off-limits until the paint is completely dry, then enjoy it.

Paneling

Paneling is ideal for many family or recreation rooms, especially those in a basement. You can effectively build a new interior shell with paneling, hiding once and for all walls that are too unattractive to redeem without considerable work. And the space behind the paneling can be treated for moisture control and insulated. Many paneling types are easily cleaned and extremely durable. The warm look of paneling makes it an attractive addition to many family room decorating schemes, both contemporary and traditional.

Do not limit your thinking to dark wood when it comes to paneling. Light, bright, colored, textured, and patterned panels are available for any number of effects. While real wood paneling and veneered wood-like paneling are all-time favorites, investigate as well the coated hardboard panels that have solid colors or different styles.

Choosing the right paneling often depends upon its durability, looks, and cost. Sheet paneling is by far the favorite for easy installation. Many sheets are constructed so that they give the illusion of plank paneling, with prefinished surfaces and grooves. The most common size is a 4 x 8 foot sheet, although some special-order sheets of 10 foot heights are available.

Plywood panels feature real wood veneers, as exotic as ebony and as rustic as sand-blasted, heavy-grain textures. The surface wood is real. Coated hardboard panels are tough and usually less costly, with surfaces that imitate the faces of nature in wood, shingle, stucco, stone and other decorative treatments. Finishes are usually easy to clean. Decorative particleboard also comes in attractive finishes.

Thickness and surface treatment determine the toughness of all of these boards, and serves as a basis for your comparison shopping.

If you want the elegance of paneling, but do not want the cost of completely encircling your family room, consider using it for an accent wall, and painting

Walls covered in a cork brick pattern are highlighted with lights hidden behind panels in a driftwood finish. Cut-outs of the paneling in cactus shapes complete this highly unusual wall treatment by designer Karl Steinhauser. Desert-like woven fabric covers the Barcalounger Recliners. (Barcalounger Recliner photo)

One accent wall of this dark paneling, with matching shelf, is all this room could comfortably handle. It becomes a dramatic background for a sculpture, and a perfect foil for the unusual seating arrangement. (Trend Line Furniture)

the other three. Four full walls of paneling often are too much for a room in any case, especially if the room tends to be dark. Another treatment is to use a chair-rail height encirclement of paneling, with or without a full accent wall. The coordinated moldings offered by most paneling manufacturers make conversion of partial walls easy.

Consider, too, whether you want the grooves of the paneling to be used conventionally, with vertical lines. This is a favorite installation since it visually adds height to a room. Other alternatives include using the paneling horizontally, or on the diagonal. The latter application calls for more cutting and fitting, so it is best reserved for the really adept.

Sheet paneling with bevels gives the feeling of planks, but has the advantage of interesting repeated grain pattern. ("Valley Forge Antique Birch" by Georgia Pacific)

Paneling applications vary according to the walls they are to cover and the nature of the material. Handy booklets abound for each of the paneling types, to show you where and how easily paneling can be installed, and give recommended care suggestions.

Panels can be directly applied to clean, smooth, dry, true wall surfaces. Old walls that are out of plumb make this application unadvisable. If you have any doubts about the suitability of the wall surface in terms of plumb or unevenness, use furring to create the proper background for attaching the paneling. If you plan to put paneling over brick, concrete, or cinder-block walls, you will want to apply a vapor barrier and perhaps insulation. This is relatively easy when you use furring strips.

The trick is to make as tight a seal as possible, so there is no leakage of either coldness or moisture. The latter can cause panels to warp once in place. The important thing to remember is that the barrier side goes closest to the inside of the room. Otherwise, the insulation can become a moisture-laden sponge, trapping room moisture behind the paneling and creating interior problems.

Insulation and vapor protection are two huge positive steps in converting a basement to a livable game room. Often, the use of insulation and a vapor barrier behind paneling is the most convenient and least costly solution to the entire mold and clamminess problem.

Measuring the room is the next step, once you have decided on the kind of paneling and method of application. Using your graph paper, draw each wall and properly position doorways, windows, and other major and minor areas that call for special treatment. Then, you can begin your assignment of paneling sheets to cover the walls. You will want to start in the least noticed corner of the room and proceed around it.

The moldings provided by the manufacturer are ingeniously designed for quick and easy application, and are as perfect a match as you are likely to find. You can use your measurements from the graph paper to determine exactly the sizes and kinds of moldings you will need.

It is always a good idea to buy moldings and paneling at the same time, to assure a close match. For the same reason, allow about 5 percent extra in your total count, to make up for any errors or imperfect pieces. In some cases, this is merely one additional sheet of paneling.

Materials

You will need standard carpenter's tools; and, follow the recommendation of the manufacturer regarding adhesives or the matched nails and moldings that are available. In addition to these, you will need to add furring to your list. 1 x 2's or 1 x 3's provide a solid base and are most often used. If your walls are not straight, you will need to have shingles for shimming the furring strips into alignment. Use 8-penny common nails if nailing the strips to studs; if putting onto a masonry wall use special steel masonry nails.

Furring Strips

Furring strips are usually applied to the walls at top edges, sides and bottom of each panel, and around any edges such as doors or windows. If using solid wood paneling, you will not need vertical strips, just horizontal strips applied on 16-inch centers. Make sure the furring is straight, so you can use it as a check for the straightness of the paneling. If you are using sheet paneling, however, you must cut furring strips to fit between the horizontals, and install them vertically. These vertical strips are placed where the edges of the sheet material fall; place horizontal strips 16 inches on center, every 48 inches for 4 x 8 sheets; lay out and draw up a furring plan for each wall before you put up the vertical furring.

Here 1x2s are spaced 16 inches apart and are nailed to studs. (Photo courtesy of Masonite Corporation)

For masonry walls you will not need to nail into studs, and you can just fur vertically every 16 inches, with horizontal strips at the floor and the ceiling to catch the tops and bottoms of the panels.

Advantages. The horizontal furring provides a base for addition of the panels, so you are no longer inhibited by the location of studs. The verticals do not need to be nailed to the studs, they merely provide support at the edges so that the joint will resist pressure. You can just cement them in place with some of the paneling adhesive. Later, when you put up the paneling, drive small nails into the vertical furring to hold it in place.

Exposed studs. When the studs are exposed you can still give the effect of furring strips by using 2 x 4's cut to length and inserted horizontally, about 24 inches apart. This is particularly helpful for solid wood paneling.

Preparation

Preparation includes allowing the paneling to become adjusted to the atmosphere of the area. Follow the manufacturer's instructions for stacking the paneling with sufficient air space around it to dry it out, and in such a way that you minimize buckling. This stage generally takes three days. Your adhesive and other materials also can be stored and acclimatized at this time. If a minimum temperature is to be maintained for use of the adhesive, make sure that the room is set for it at this stage. You may also want to use a dehumidifier to take out any residue of moisture that has remained in the room after insulation has been added.

In every move throughout the paneling operation, including this first stage, be especially careful not to mar the panel surfaces. For instance, stack panels face to face and back to back to prevent scratching.

Laying out the panels is cumbersome, but necessary to make sure that grain variations are pleasing and attractive from one panel to its neighbor. You can achieve uniformity in many cases by up-ending alternate panels along the walls. Remove molding before placing your paneling for a better approximation of how the paneling will fit flush to the walls.

To keep track of your layout, number the back of each panel. Record its position on your layout or directly on the wall section it is to cover. If you are re-using moldings, mark them on the back so you can tell where they are to be reinstalled.

Installation

Attaching the paneling is done with either adhesive or nails. Here are the steps that are generally recommended, although you should follow exactly the manufacturer's recommendations for the paneling you have chosen.

1. Cutting and fitting panels starts with these dimensions: Panels should be ¼ inch less than actual ceiling height. Measure all along the wall to see if there is more that a ¼ inch variation. If so, cut each panel to fit separately. If not, take the smallest measurement and cut all panels to that length. Standard ceiling and floor moldings will cover panel height variations up to 2 inches. Allow at least 1/32 inch (the thickness of a dime) between panels. Never force panels into position; they need a bit of space for expansion.

2. Most cutting can be done either with fast power tools, or hand sawing. Use the manufacturer's suggestions for appropriate blades and techniques. Usually, panels are cut face up with hand tools,

Be careful when cutting panels to avoid damage to the finish. Circular saw is used with panels face down, because blade tips cut upwards. Use a compass to trace irregularities where the panels must fit; then cut paneling along these lines in order to fit panels into particular areas, such as next to this brick facing.

Use a ⅝ or ¾ inch drill to start on corners of a small cutout area; follow up with a keyhole saw; or (4) use a power jig saw to cut exact cutout lines.

and face down with power saws to achieve the best edges. These are then dress-roughed with a plane, file, or sandpaper. If you are cutting face down, be sure to provide a surface that will not mar the paneling front.

3. Start in one of the least-noticed corners, to actually fit panels. Position the panel about 1 inch from the corner edge, and use a scribing compass with one leg following the wall contour, the other scribing a line along the panel edge from top to bottom. Make sure that the panel is plumb, using a level vertically along the outside edge, before scribing. A china-marking pencil for scribing is recommended for many paneling products. Fit the scribed panel into position (1/32 inch from the corner), and again adjust and check for plumb. Follow this same procedure at each new corner, to make sure the first panel is absolutely straight. The other panels are lined up with this one.

4. Before attaching, tack the panel in position at the top and once again check plumbness. Tack inconspicuously into grooves, preferably where molding will cover nail marks.

5. Use shingles or other supports at the bottom to hold panels in position while lining them up.

6. For adhesive application, follow the manufacturer's suggestions. Usually, the panel is tacked once again after adhesive is applied at the top, then paneling is pressed into adhesive. After a 15 to 20 minute interval, apply final pressure with a hammer or mallet, cushioning with a padded block of wood.

Prefinished panel is moved into position over the furring strips and imemdiately pressed into position. Uniform hand pressure is used.

Two nails at the top maintain panel position. Leave heads exposed for easy removal later.

A 1/8-inch thick, continuous ribbon of adhesive is applied to clean furring strips and other surfaces where the panel edges will go.

A padded block of wood and a hammer or mallet are used, after a 15-to-20 minute interval, to reapply pressure and give the final bond.

A scrap of carpet is put under the hammer to protect the paneling surface while top nails are removed. (Photos courtesy of Masonite Corporation)

7. For nail application, start the nailing from the center of the panel to avoid bulging; never work from edges first. Spacing of nails varies according to the kind of paneling, so check which is best for yours. For instance, Wal-Lite calls for spacing 8 inches for intermediate strips or studs, and 4 inches around the edges of each panel.

8. To handle spaces between panels, paint or use a marker pen to color wide lines on the wall or furring behind the panels to match and disguise spaces. Then, lightly drive a 3d nail 12 inches from the ceiling, in the center, and 12 inches up from the floor flush to the attached panel. Line up the next panel to these nails, attach the next panel, and remove the "spacer" nails which have given you your 1/32 inch gaps.

9. For piecing at the end of the wall, place the rough edge in the corner, and the finished edge into the room.

10. To make a door or window cut, measure from top to bottom, and plan your cut so that it is seamed over the top edge. It is easier to fit two cut-out halves than to make an accurate window or door cut in a whole panel.

11. To cut around electrical outlets, check your measurements very carefully. Then, remember to pull the outlet box forward to compensate for panel thickness. A quick trick is to chalk the edge of the outlet box. Then, carefully fit the panel in place. Strike the face of the panel several times with the heel of your hand to transfer the chalk outline to the back of the panel. Drill pilot holes in the corner of the outlined square, then saw the fitted opening.

12. Finish all paneling, nailing, or gluing before applying moldings. If you must hammer something on the front of the paneling, use a block such as a 2 x 4 x 12-inch wrapped in soft material (like carpet scraps), to disperse the weight and avoid hammer marks.

13. Apply moldings. The matched, ingenious moldings designed by paneling manufacturers are a snap to use, and make many less-than-perfect jobs look totally professional.

Consider other paneling or wood applications for an original look. While there is a paneling type for almost any look you might want to achieve, for a different approach investigate the new barnboard planks or simulated shingles; these have a depth and texture that are more realistic than in conventional paneling. Made by manufacturers who have kept the do-it-yourselfer in mind, these are often easily applied, using some of the techniques similar to installing paneling. The mounting accessories that are provided also make the job easier.

If you decide to try rough-hewn walls, make sure that your children will not be rubbing up against the splintery surfaces.

A rugged look is achieved with this shake-and-shingle wall. It is made from Easy Panels, with single real shakes attached to horizontal panels 16¾ inches high by 4 feet long. Eight panels cover 37 square feet, and can be used indoors or out. (Shakertown Panels)

Stone and Brick

Simulated stones and brick wall treatments are other means of achieving interesting and three-dimensional walls. Some are even designed for use behind free-standing fireplaces, acting as an insulating barrier. Others have the look of lasting durability, but are made of manmade materials for decorative effect only, unsuitable for behind fireplaces.

Since natural materials are extremely heavy, the use of the manmade substitutes puts far less load on floors or walls. And, it is literally impossible to tell the difference with some of the new products.

Brick

Do-it-yourself brick walls can be composition or slabs of actual bricks. They come in sheets or in indi-

Decorative brick is effective, and lightweight. An adhesive mortar is trowelled onto the surface, and substitute brick is easily laid on it. A) Mortar is trowelled on surface. B) Bricks slide into position in whatever pattern is to be used, and wiggled for a good bond with the mortar-adhesive. C) Mortar is smoothed between bricks once they are positioned. D) A final coat of protective sealer is applied when the job is dry and finished. (Z-Brick photos)

vidual units, with corner units precast for easy adaptation to your design. The methods of attaching include use of grout especially designed for them, and standard panel applications. Bricks are available in different colors and styles, which combine with grouting material for highly individual effects.

Stone

Manmade stone walls are offered in sheet and unit systems for easy application. They are good choices when you want the textural impact of this kind of material, without the demanding redness and regularity of a brick wall. The larger, free-form stone shapes, with their muted tones of beige and grey, might be just the accent a room needs.

Wall Coverings

Wall coverings, including wallpaper, are the other grand illusion creators in family rooms. Imagine the impact of a powerful paper pattern of sunshine-drenched daisies brightening up a dark corner, or matched upholstery and wallpaper in a wildly contemporary geometric drawing the eye's attention. You even can choose period wall coverings to give the air of authenticity to a nostalgic turn-of-the-century room, or an Early American decor. More understated coverings include plain, textured colors.

Choices are almost endless. The greatest improvement in wall coverings in recent years has been in the introduction of strippable, or easily applied self-stick papers, and highly durable washable (even scrubbable, in some cases!) papers that will resist even crayon markings.

Wall coverings can be used for all walls, or part of the walls only. A total treatment is an effective way of disguising odd angles and other protuberances that need unification. If walls are slightly marred, then a patterned or textured paper can hide the imperfections. For larger areas that are uneven, prepare the wall as you might for painting, by patching and priming areas to assure a good bond.

Consider, also, using color-coordinated wall coverings in different patterns to set off special areas. For instance, you might opt for a sedate stripe for the main family room area, and a colorful plaid or floral that is color-matched for the entertainment area. Many wall covering manufacturers include collections with this kind of coordination already worked out for you.

Another treatment combines a wall covering with matched fabric for upholstery or curtains. This is a simple solution to walls that are broken up with uneven windows, or any other area whose parts need to be visually tied together.

Fabric drapes match the wallcovering, to cover a sliding door. ("Dundee" from Strahan, photo from the Wallcovering Industry Bureau)

Overscaled patterns are dramatic when used with contemporary furniture. This pattern takes careful matching and requires more wall covering than would a smaller pattern, but gives much greater effect. (Recliner from Barcalounger)

Your wall covering distributor will guide you in choosing the right kind of covering for the existing walls that you plan to decorate. Follow his advice as well in the choice of paste (if the paper is not pre-pasted), and any necessary preparation steps.

Pretrimmed and prepasted coverings are the easiest to use for border motifs, since you need not interfere with the painting job that has already been done. If you plan to combine painting and papering in the same area (such as using paper as a decorative border around one area, or merely on an accent wall), you are better off painting first. It is easier to touch up a paint job than it is to remove spilled paint from your wall covering.

Pattern

Preferences are highly personal, so explore the variety of designs available, and pick the one you like best. Consider the effect of the pattern and texture on the walls to be covered, and choose the pattern that will be most flattering to that space.

Plaids are obvious straight-match wallcoverings. This one is used effectively to cover sides of the bookcases as well as the walls. It has an easy-care surface that just needs wiping for cleanup. (Con-Tact Brand Self Adhesive Vinyl by Comark Plastics)

Another element in choosing wall covering is to know what kind of matching occurs from one strip to another. Some patterns are so random that the covering can be reversed with no visible signs on the wall. The majority of patterns, however, demand careful matching. The types of matching are:

- Random matches. As described above, these look well no matter how each panel relates to its neighbor, and are simplest to apply. Stripes, grasscloth, burlap, and all-over textures are examples.

- Straight matches. The pattern of one strip must be joined with a matching design at the same height in the adjacent panel.

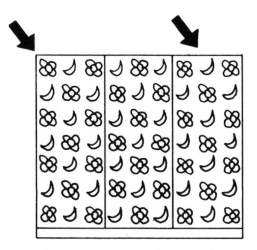

These strips show a drop-match pattern. Every other strip is the same at the top. (Drawing courtesy of National Decorating Products Association)

- Drop matches. Like a herringbone weave, these patterns depend upon the continuation of the match at alternating distances from the ceiling. The pattern matches at the same horizontal level on alternate strips. Sometimes, the effect is one of a pattern on the diagonal.

Almost all patterns except random ones have repeats. These are complete sections of design that are repeated once again. To match up large repeats, you will have to allow for more waste than for matching small repeats. So, work out the general yardage required to cover the area you have in mind, and then follow your dealer's advice on the amount of extra covering you will need to accommodate repeats and to allow for hems. Buy more than enough wall covering right at the beginning, to be assured of an exact match for the whole job. Any scraps can be used in a multitude of decorative ways.

Tools

You will need a yardstick, scissors, stepladder, razor knife, seam roller, wide wall-scraper, string, chalk and plumb line weight, smoothing brush, large sponge and bucket, sandpaper and sandpaper block for preparing walls, drop cloth, screwdriver, and a good raised working surface covered with craft paper, or drop cloth.

You may need or want some other accessories, such as a water tray, depending upon the kind of paper you have chosen. Most supplies you probably have already, with the exception of inexpensive tools specifically for applying wall covering.

Preparation

To prepare your room, follow the guidelines for installing paneling or painting. You need to protect furniture, and you also need a good workspace for applying paste, if your pattern is not prepasted.

Do any painting of moldings now, and let them dry. Remove all switch plates, outlet plates, and light fixtures on the wall. Trim untrimmed wall covering, and inspect each roll for defects. Do whatever repairs are necessary to the old wall to assure a good bond. This would include smoothing any cracks, cleaning away any soil, or priming if necessary.

Know the application techniques before you make any moves to prepare the pasting part of this operation. Once you are thoroughly familiar with the methods of applying wall covering, you can intersperse the steps of moistening the paper and hanging it, so that some strips are getting ready while you are hanging earlier ones. This is the secret of swift wall covering hanging. However, take it slow and easy enough to make sure your strips are aligned right, and check your handiwork as you go along.

1. Start in the least noticeable corner. Measure the width of the strip minus ½ inch from the corner. Mark this measurement near ceiling, near baseboard, and in the center of the wall. Tack a chalked plumb line over the mark that is nearest the wall, and snap chalk line onto wall.

2. Your first strip will be lined up along this line, towards the corner, and wrapped around the corner the extra ½ inch. You turn the corner with the paper so that if the corner is not plumb, all of it is covered with paper.

3. Cut your first strip with a 3-inch extra edge at the top and 3-inch edge at the bottom (from ceiling line to baseboard). Paper generally looks best when an

Starting from a door or corner, measure one strip-width, less ½ inch, to the right and make a plumb line mark, snapping plumb line on the wall.

Cut your first strip, allowing three extra inches at top and bottom. Match the pattern and cut two more; hang all three before cutting more.

entire motif begins below the ceiling line, rather than starting in the middle of one. So, start your top cut three inches above the main motif, and the bottom cut three inches below the wall length.

4. Wet prepasted strips, or apply paste to unpasted strips. Here are methods of achieving this:

(a) Prepasted strips are easily hung by using a water tray. The tray is filled and placed below the wall section where the paper covering is to hang. Set your ladder diagonally in front of it. Loosely re-roll the first strip from the bottom to the top with the pattern side in, pasted side out. Submerge rolled strip the recommended time length. When

Pull strip from water tray or apply water to paste with a brush on a table, with pattern side down. Fold as shown, paste to paste, and set aside if strippable, or hang immediately after folding (booking). Prepare second and third strip the same way.

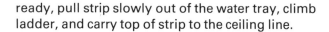

Roll up strip, pasted side out and place in a water-filled tray. Weight the strip with a table knife inside so it is completely submerged in the water.

Using a drop cloth, place water box at baseboard. Slowly unroll wet strip, soaked appropriate time length. Align with plumb line and hang.

Unfold top part of strip only, and position it near the ceiling leaving 3 inches to trim later. Line strip up with right edge on the plumb line.

ready, pull strip slowly out of the water tray, climb ladder, and carry top of strip to the ceiling line.

(b) Another method with prepasted strips is to use a table to soften the paste. Use a brush to generously apply water to the inside of the strip, laid over the table pattern side down. Fold the top of the strip toward the center, paste to paste. Never crease the folds. Fold up the bottom half in the same way, so that both edges meet at the center. This is called "booking." Loosely roll the folded strip and lay it aside for the length of time recommended by the manufacturer. You also can combine the water tray and booking techniques, if booked strips are easiest for you to handle.

(c) Unpasted wall coverings have the paste applied with a brush on a table, and then are booked to allow the paste to set up, as described above. Be sure to cover every area with paste; a figure-eight motion is recommended for even distribution of paste.

5. Hang the first pasted strip by placing it high on the wall so that it overlaps the ceiling joint approximately 3 inches. Use the plumb line for lining up, and allow the other edge to wrap around in the corner. Using your wide brush, give the upper section of the strip a couple of horizontal strokes at the ceiling line to force it into ceiling corner. Follow with downward strokes going from the center to

Use a ruler with knife or razor blade to trim top, bottom, and around any doors or windows. Wipe off paste with wet sponge, and roll down edges with a seam roller, unless paper manufacturer specifies otherwise (flocked papers, for example).

each side, to smooth the paper securely onto the wall. Check your lining up by stepping back before you use the same techniques for the lower half of the strip (you can leave it booked while you attach the top half).

6. When covering is positioned even with the plumb line, go over the entire strip to make sure all air bubbles are removed, and that the ½ inch overlap is firmly secured at the corner. Handle the strip in the center, not by tugging the edges, so that edges are not stretched.

7. Use your wall scraper as a guide for trimming the extra 3 inches at top and bottom. Place scraper on wall, and cut against ceiling.

8. Line up the second strip, making sure that this strip matches the pattern of your first strip. Apply or soften glue, and attach. Use the same techniques for additional strips.

9. Electrical outlets are easily handled, once you know how. The most important factor is to TURN OFF THE CURRENT BEFORE YOU PAPER THEM. With metallic papers especially, this advice may be lifesaving, since the metallic part of the paper may conduct the electric current. You have already removed the face plate, so hang the wall covering directly over the outlet. Then, with a single edge razor blade, cut away the paper covering the outlet or switch and replace the plate or fixture. Cover the plate with scraps to match the wall covering before putting it back.

10. Inside corners call for realignment of the covering. You line up the strip on the old wall with the last hung panel, but line up the same strip on the new wall with a new plumb line. To do this, cut the paper and overlap it at the corner, to make sure that the edge on the new wall is plumb. Start by measuring ½ inch less than the width of panel that went around the corner, and marking a plumb line at that point on the new wall. Then, butt the portion of the new strip to the last strip on the old wall, press firmly into the corner, and smooth. On the

With a wet sponge, smooth strip working from center to edges. Unfold bottom, align it with plumb line and smooth. Small bubbles disappear with drying.

Measure around corner and mark a plumb line ½ inch less than panel width. Line up panel with last panel and overlap into corner, then cut strip ½ inch in from second wall. Line up right hand side with new plumb line, and overlap it with cut part in corner, matching pattern.

new wall, cut the full length of the strip with a scraper and razor ½ inch out from the corner. Line up the cut-off part with the new plumb line you've made, so that it overlaps the covered corner and is flush with the plumb line. If special overlapping adhesive is necessary with your wall covering, apply it at this point in the corner, and use your seam roller.

11. Outside corners are wrapped after a snip has been made in the overhang at ceiling and floor for ease of handling. Since the corner is probably not plumb, hang the longest wall first, so that any slight nonalignment on the second wall is on the smallest wall. If the corner is badly out of line, follow the directions for rehanging a new plumb panel for inside corners, and start on the second wall afresh.

12. If your covering ends at a corner (outside or inside), cut back ¼ inch from the edge to eliminate fraying or peeling from the edge.

13. Doors, windows, and fireplaces are easier to work around than you might think. Merely fit your covering right over the edges when you come to one, and then cut excess away with scissors, making a diagonal cut to the corners. Finish up by trimming with your scraper and razor blade. Matching sections from full-width strips can be used above and below these cut-outs.*

Allow at least one inch overage in papering up to a door or window frame. Use matching panels above and below windows. (Photos from Imperial Wallcoverings, a Collins & Aikman Co.)

*For more specifics on types of paper and fabric wall coverings and their applications, see *Wall Coverings and Decoration* by Banov, a *Successful* book.

Wall coverings will work in any family-room area, so long as you are prepared to pave the way for them. With old walls that are really unsuitable, you can put up plasterboard as the base. Or, if old wallpaper is firmly adhered to the wall and you are careful not to overlap on the same seams, you often can paper over old wall coverings. Keep in mind that the thinner papers, especially the metallics, allow for more show-through of the material behind them, and take greater care in application. But all wall coverings are relatively easy to apply, and give an exciting finished look to a room.

Problem walls with non-receptive surfaces can now be papered with a special wall lining that bridges minor cracks and recesses. The 24-inch wide material is applied with ready-mix vinyl adhesive and in turn is covered with whatever decorative wall covering you wish. (Collins & Aikman Co., Imperial Wallcoverings)

Murals

Murals are specialized wall coverings that aid in optically enlarging your space. By creating the illusion of a scene with depth, the wall upon which they are placed seems to recede.

Most murals are designed to fit on an average-sized wall. Additional panels of plain paper with the same background as the mural are used to fill in below, above, and on either side of the mural if necessary. Manufacturers provide the directions for properly hanging their artwork walls, which generally begin with centering the design on the wall to be covered.

This mural fills the whole wall, reduces the number of furnishings and accessories needed, and reinforces the period decor. (Classic Connoisseur Wall Coverings, Inc.)

This sophisticated room uses Fieldcrest "Missoni" sheets in Art Deco and striped patterns on the walls. Sheeting is easy to apply to walls, using the wallpaper method, and you can put up great sweeps of fabric without seams when using large-size sheets. (Fieldcrest)

Some murals are designed to be used in conjunction with furniture, and have the main portion of the decoration at above-furniture height. These work well behind seating units or low bookcases. Others are meant to be seen from floor to ceiling. Your furniture arrangement will best determine which of these types suits your family room.

In addition to your furniture arrangement, take into consideration the altered dimensional effect that a mural will create. For instance, in a long and narrow room, the wall you want to visually expand would be one of the side walls. A mural placed on the end wall of a long and narrow room succeeds only in making the room seem longer and narrower.

Popular mural choices are those that give a feeling of open spaces for basement family rooms, and they often are easily incorporated into the general room theme. Examples are murals with garden scene motifs, harbor view motifs, or some of the photographic murals that emulate the great outdoors. Pop art murals are also grand favorites, especially for party family rooms. Some come with metallic backgrounds and brilliant color.

Fabric Walls

Fabrics are available in wide sheets for easy application on walls. If your windows make a dominant wall treatment unsuitable, but you want the softness and style of fabric in the room, investigate fabrics for application to all walls or merely some of them. Or, use a fabric that matches your wall covering to unify your window treatment.

The three main ways of adhering fabric to walls are: applying it as you would wallpaper; stapling; and, shirring it for a softer look.

Wallpaper Methods

These are the same measuring and installation steps covered under wallpaper techniques. Special pastes are used for adhering fabric, but the steps taken are the same. You will need to use a fabric with little show-through (burlap and felt are popular) since it should give the look and feel of substance on the wall. Loose weaves are least handy to work with, while tightly woven fabrics give wonderful effects with relatively little work.

Trim the selvages that do not fit the matching of the patterns, and either double the edges over (which creates a little bump on the wall) or cut through overlapped fabric at seams for the kind of match seam that is so successful with regular wallpaper. Trim hems at the top and bottom as is done with wallpaper, always using a good sharp razor edge. One advantage of using fabric is that you can use decorative bindings to cover hems and seams with great effect...and to cover less-than-perfect jobs.

Stapling

Stapling is another quick and easy way of applying fabric to walls. With this method, you can staple into many walls directly with a staple gun. To guard against cracking, put a strip of masking tape where staples will

The fabric used on the back of this Milo Baughman designed furniture for Thayer Coggin is coordinated with wool-ribbed fabric used on the back wall to emphasize architectural feeling of the furniture. Stapling is one system of attaching fabrics quickly to the wall. (Thayer Coggin)

go into the wall. If your walls will not take stapling, then add furring strips first, and staple the fabric to them. Attach furring strips around the entire perimeter of the wall area to be covered, around windows or doors, and any other protuberances.

Open sheet hems and steam press. Match the repeats and stitch sheets together allowing ½-inch seams when more than one sheet is needed to cover a wall. Then cut sheets into lengths 6 inches longer than the wall height.

Establish a plumb line on the wall, to make sure your sheet pattern is properly lined up. Use push pins to temporarily hold the sheeting in place while you line it up for stapling. Allow 3 inches extra at top and bottom, and begin in a corner by stapling or pinning the sheeting to ceiling-joint furring strips at wide intervals to hold it in place.

Return to the corner, and staple or push-pin sheeting to hold it in place down corner furring. Then starting at corner, staple across the top furring strip placing staples 1 inch apart, smoothing out wrinkles as you go, and turning edges under. Next, work down the sides, stapling down both sides as you go. Finish the bottom edge last. Cover your staples, unless they do not show due to the pattern you have chosen, with decorative molding, ribbon, braid, or welting.

Shirring

Shirred fabric walls have by far the softest look and can be very effective. Start by attaching furring strips or masking tape to walls where shirred panels will be anchored—the top, bottom, and edges. Allow a 3½-inch hem at each end of the panels after pattern matching. You will need at least two times the amount of the wall to be covered in fabric width, in order to achieve the proper shirring fullness.

Cable cord will hold the shirring at the top and bottom, strung through a casing seam in the fabric. To shir fabric, turn a 3½-inch hem at top and bottom. Run a stitch 1½ inches from turned hem, and another 1 inch below that. Cable cord is inserted in the 1-inch seam casing below the leading seam.

Next, gather the fabric along the length of the cable cord at the top and bottom, distributing it evenly. Tack it in position along the wall, before stapling it permanently, to be certain that the shirring is even. Attach the cable cord to the wall at the top and staple shirred fabric to wall. Finish by repeating the process at the bottom, and the panels are in place.

Use Mirrors to Multiply Effects

Mirrors are magic makers for most rooms: they can visually double space, make a small space seem more open, and even hide some architectural flaws when used properly. The trick is to understand how to use them.

Strange as it seems, many people forget to consider what will be reflected when deciding where to use mirrors. That is the first consideration in placing them. They also must look well where they are placed, so keep both factors in mind.

Always place a mirror in position to check what it will reflect before permanently installing it. The difference of a mere few inches may turn an unpleasant reflection into one of beauty. Check to see what is reflected both when seated and when standing. Then, plan the positioning of the mirror for the angle from which it is most likely to be viewed. A favorite reflection is one through a window on the opposite wall, although other vignettes are equally attractive.

Safety is another important factor in placing mirrors. Make sure they cannot easily be dislodged or hazardously bumped into, and that they do not create confusion. For instance, make sure that a mirror that reflects a doorway cannot be mistaken for the doorway itself.

Consider using mirror walls to visually alter the proportions of a room into more pleasing scale. For instance, a hallway can appear doubled with the addition of a mirror wall along one side. A narrow room will seem wider with the addition of a mirror wall along the long side. Be careful not to use mirror walls in positions where they will emphasize the lack of scale of a room. For instance, do not place a mirrored treatment at the end of a long room, since it will only make it seem doubly long and narrow.

Be free-wheeling in considering locations for mirrors. Small ones can be used to reflect almost anything. These are easily incorporated into arrange-

Note how the mirror placed above the built-in fireplace picks up a beautiful outside view. You get two views at the same time: the fire, and the greenery outside. (Room designed by Nick Grande for Stratford Co.)

Mirror tiles create the illusion of doubled space and are easiest for a do-it-yourselfer to handle. Note how grand this stairway looks with the doubled effect. Mirrors also save on lighting bills, since they increase both natural and artificial light. (PPG Industries, Inc. mirrors)

ments of other objects or paintings used on the wall. One good use of mirrors is in the returns of deep window frames, which gives the illusion of twice the window surface when viewed from slightly off center.

Tiles

Mirror tiles need to be securely mounted on a surface, and come with self-stick backings as well as mounting attachments. You will find mirror tiles in clear styles as well as some with decorations or special effects such as antiquing. Less costly than good plate mirrors, these are ideal for inexpensive do-it-yourself applications. You can stretch their impact and use even less tiles by separating the tiles and using them in attractive designs. For instance, add a mirror strip or alternating strips to the wall. Also use tiles in a checkerboard pattern instead of in a solid cluster.

Whole Walls

Mirror walls are somewhat expensive, but well worth the value in lack of distortion. They are heavy enough to be safely installed permanently, and require virtually no care once in place. A good mirror wall will require only occasional cleaning, while giving you years of use. Since good, permanent installation is essential, you might save in the long run by having professionals handle the mirrors. They are used to working with mirrors without scratching or breaking them when in large sheet form.

Furniture

Mirrors incorporated into furniture also add zest to a family room. One favorite application is the use of a mirrored background for a bar storage unit placed behind the bar. Glasses and bottles plus other decorative

objects are wonderfully displayed on shelves placed before the mirrored backgrounds.

Some storage units come with mirrored fronts, offering disguised storage while adding decorative impact. Among these are units that are narrow shelving with bi-fold, long and narrow mirrored doors. Other units combine mirror surfaces with solid materials.

Wall Coverings

Metallic wall coverings can be used to substitute for more expensive mirror walls when you want a softened mirror effect. Relatively inexpensive self-stick materials are available for application on small surfaces. Metallic patterned wall coverings are a bit trickier to apply than regular wall coverings, since they show every imperfection of the material beneath them, and can be scratched. However, they give a shiny, reflective surface at less cost.

Other mirror-like coverings include such exotic but readily available materials as aluminum foil. It can be applied to walls with wallpaper paste, allowing the wrinkles that are bound to occur to become part of the overall textural interest of the wall covering. Metallic sheets that are formed, such as those that are found on the ceilings of turn-of-the-century buildings, are coming back into vogue as both ceiling and wall coverings. Even corrugated galvanized steel is used in its unfinished state for handsome metallic-looking wall covering. Both of these latter materials take great care in application, since the edges tend to be very sharp. By looking around, you can find a metallic/mirrorlike material for almost any need or effect.

8. Ceiling and Window Treatments

The finishing details covered in the last two chapters are the most important ones in giving character to your basic room. Those covered in this chapter work hand-in-hand with the wall covering and flooring you have chosen, which in some cases will dominate and set the tone for the entire room. In any case, you will want to be sure that the windows and ceiling in your family/recreation room are as well-plotted as the other decorative elements.

Windows

Window treatments always require care in planning. If you have large windows, they need convenient coverings, and must be integrated into the room decor. They may be the major design statement in the entire room. On the other hand, small windows take just as much planning, to insure their impact. Here are some of the considerations in choosing the best window treatments for your family room.

A full window treatment with draperies, a valence, and glass or casement curtains that diffuse light, gives softness to this rather formal family room. Fabric is matched on tablecloth and upholstery. Carpet in two colors softly repeats the choice of fabric pattern used throughout. (World "Endless Shadows" Anso nylon carpet, Allied Chemical Corp.)

1. Match your window treatment to the total room design. For example, with an Early American room, consider painted curtain rods and rings that match your woodwork, rustic shutters, or casual café curtains. Unless your room is relatively formal, avoid stately treatments such as formal valences and draperies.

Strong supergraphics are repeated in this shirred-top-and-bottom and tied drapery treatment at the windows, creating diamond effects. The colorful carpet in a geometric works well with the sleek wall and window treatment. (Carpet by Viking in Allied Chemical Corp. Anso Nylon fiber)

2. Emphasize or minimize windows according to their relationship to the total room scheme. For example, large patterned draperies on a mainly glass window wall may overwhelm every other room element. A more suitable treatment might be wall-to-wall curtains that echo the wall color, or are in an understated neutral color. Another common problem, especially in basements, are windows that are smaller than desired. These demand a treatment that makes them look more prominent than they are. One solution would be extending the curtains or shades for small windows out on either side, to make them look wider. Or, use café cur-

There is a shade to suit almost any window, as illustrated by this shade—it can be draped canopy-fashion or pulled taut, and can be cleaned in the tub. The shade stripes key the entire color scheme; room design by Peg Walker. (Stauffer Chemical Co. shade, photo from the Window Shade Manufacturers Association)

tains below the window to give the illusion that the windows extend to the floor.

3. Unify window treatments so that each window enhances the impact of the other windows. In addition to using the same materials, artfully plan your treatments so that the curtain length and heading heights are uniform. Use of the same treatment on a series of windows unifies the total room design through pleasant repetition.

4. Make sure your window treatment does not interfere with the opening and closing of the windows, and that the window treatment itself will be convenient to open and close. Will shades clear the top of French doors? Should drapes go to one side or both sides? Which side should draw drapes pull back to? Are pulleys located where they will be easy to reach with your furniture placement?

5. Make sure window treatments are attractive both day and night. If you plan to have a window covered most of the time (perhaps to hide an unpleasant view), then your closed window treatment is most important. However, if you plan to spend a good deal of time in the room during the day time and want the view, your treatment must be attractive with the window exposed. Tiebacks and valances give open window treatments a more finished look, and should be given greater consideration when a room is used often in the daytime.

6. Check that your window treatment looks well both inside and out. There is nothing worse than an attractive house with an ugly curtain or shade backs blaring from the windows. Many shades, shutters, blinds, and fabric treatments look good

from both sides. The addition of glass curtains and linings can solve most problems where the treatment you have chosen for inside is not as attractive as you would like from the outside.

7. Use window treatments that help solve insulation, privacy, and sun control problems. Although any window treatment will add up to savings in all these areas, some are more efficient than others.

Popular window treatments include curtains and draperies, shades, blinds, shutters, and bare window treatments. Combinations of these materials are often the best solutions for stylized window treatments.

Try combining materials and investigating the various hanging arrangements around. Hardware choices are endless, as are the types of materials used for window treatments. Many are easy-care so that they stay good-looking for many years with a minimum of effort. Listed here are some of the considerations in choosing one type versus another, and tips on installing them.

Curtains and Drapes

These add softness to windows. You can match a favorite wallpaper or fabric used in upholstery, or achieve a unified look by using the same fabric on windows and walls.

There are curtain styles that will coordinate well with any furniture style, since curtains are a traditional means of covering windows. Casement curtains (sometimes called glass or sash curtains) are made of softly gathered sheer fabric and hang directly in front of the window to soften daylight. Draw curtains can be opened and closed, and are generally more opaque than casements. Drapery panels act as frames for windows and cannot be drawn. These are often used in conjunction with draw draperies or casement curtains, and give a more formal look.

Less formal curtains include shirred, ruffled, and café styles. Shirred curtains are gathered directly on the rods, and are simple to make. Ruffled curtains include criss-crossing types used with tiebacks, and are feminine and frilly in most cases. Café curtains hang straight from exposed rings on an exposed rod, and can be used in tiers to cover the entire window or to cover only part of the window. These are often used in combination with shutters.

No matter what the style, careful measuring is a must for installing curtains or draperies. First, decide whether you want the fabric to extend to the sill, window apron, or floor. Allow room for clearance of carpeting and do not use floor-length draperies if they would interfere with baseboard heating.

At the top, curtains can be suspended from the ceiling, from the inside of the window frame, or from the frame itself. If you want to make a window seem larger, use rod extenders to carry your rods to either side of the window frame. Then you can secure the rod to the frame itself without having to put holes into the wall. Figure in the amount of space needed to accommodate the curtain on either side of the window when it is drawn back. This is usually about one foot on either side for picture windows.

Take measurements for each window, even if you think they are all alike. Use a good steel measuring tape or carpenter's rule, and write down each measurement as you take it. Always re-check, because an error at this stage will cause much grief later. Remember to add the length of the return to your width dimension if the treatment you have chosen calls for a rod that curves around at the sides.

Quality pointers in choosing curtain fabric include resistance to sun damage, washability, good finishing of seams, and fullness of gathering or pleats. Generally, fabric should be at least 2 times the width of space it is to cover, and even more for lightweight fabrics. Check to see if you can take advantage of the ready-made curtains and draperies available, to save yourself both time and money. An alternate plan is to use the made-to-measure products, which are somewhat more expensive than ready-mades, but less than custom draperies. Your best savings come from making curtains or draperies yourself, taking full advantage of the pleating tapes and accessories that reduce this job to straight-seam sewing in many cases.

Shades

Window shades are an effective and fanciful means of decorating. They can be ornate, with the use of fabrics and patterns, or sleek and streamlined. Opaque and semi-opaque styles are available for sunlight control. Use them alone or in combination with shutters, or curtains. Like curtains, they work best for windows that are to be either totally covered or totally revealed, since with shades you cannot use half-measures to regulate sun flow as you can with blinds.

Decorative edgings and do-it-yourself trimmings make shades easy to customize. Kits are available to laminate fabrics to specially designed window shade styles, or this can be done professionally for you. Other elaborate effects are achieved with roll shades in woven wood, rattan, bamboo, or other strongly textured materials.

Most shades almost disappear when rolled up, which has advantages and disadvantages. They do not interfere with a view when rolled, which may be just

Cedar paneling and hand-hewn beams from U.S. Plywood, painted white, act as the frame for the series of shades in a textured spice pattern. The floor-to-ceiling shades look good raised, lowered or between. (Emily Malino design for the Window Shade Manufacturers Association)

Handsome rustic furniture for an equally rustic window treatment. Here, matchstick blinds in a tortoise pattern unify a corner window and become an interesting part of the room. ("Penthouse" furniture by Stratford Company)

what you want. On the other hand, you may require more window dressing if your rolled shades leave the window looking too bare. One solution is to suspend shade panels on either side of the window that remain down, giving a finished look, while the shades over the window are raised to let in the view. Or, combine shades with curtains or shutter treatments.

Measuring accurately for shades is very important. At the top, start shades from the ceiling, frame outer edge, or inside the window frame. At the bottom, shades can extend to the sill, apron, or floor. Remember to allow for the bulk of the shade itself and recess it down from the ceiling or window top for any needed clearance. Allow an additional foot of shade beyond its desired lowest dimension so that you will not over-extend the shade when pulling it down.

Shades placed within the window frame allow light to show at either side. If that look does not appeal to you, mount the shades to the window frame front, allowing a 1¼-inch overlap of shade on either side of the window to avoid light showing through. The addition of a heading will allow you to extend shades on either side of a window to whatever width your overall design demands.

Your choice of brackets is one of the most crucial decisions in making your shade treatment look professional. Decorated shades look tacky when rolled with a conventional standard mount, so that the underside of the shade is exposed at the top. For a sleek look, use a reverse mount, and a reverse roll so that the rolled part does not face the room. Another method of solving this problem is to use a double bracket. It allows you to add a discreet heading which covers a standard mounted shade, to the outer bracket.

Shades are also available that raise from the window bottom, but these are best left to professional installation. Do keep this type in mind as the possible solution to a difficult window-covering problem.

While you can create a unifying and dramatic look by covering two small windows with one large shade, this limits your ability to regulate the light. Using a series of matched shades that can be drawn to various lengths is an effective means of unifying windows on a wall, and gives greater flexibility.

Blinds

Window blinds are decorative as well as functional, and offer the greatest versatility when it comes to light control. Conventional Venetian blinds are available in easily cleaned metal, or can be laminated with fabric for a custom look in combination with matched draperies or alone. Sleek new thin Venetian blinds are available in a wide range of colors and also can be laminated with fabrics. Where light control is a factor, blinds are usually the best solution.

A very contemporary window treatment! Streamlined blinds that take up less space than curtains or drapes, and are narrower than conventional Venetian blinds. Soft beige color on the blinds echos the wallcovering main color and beige background on main furniture pieces. (Imperial Wallcovering, Chromcraft furniture, Collins & Aikman carpeting)

Vertical window blinds were once pretty limited to use by decorators for commercial installations, but have become increasingly popular with homeowners in recent times. They give a contemporary look to the window, with panels of blinds running from top to bottom instead of horizontally. The blinds are rotated right to left, and gather to each side instead of pulling up.

Fanciful fabrics and metallic treatments are available on vertical blinds, as well as solid colors and interesting textures. Some vertical blinds are designed to take an insert of either wallpaper or fabric to match the rest of the room decor. By choosing the right fabric or mural effects, you can create a picture wall for when the blinds are closed, and still pull the decoration entirely out of the way of the window when you want a view.

As with shades, the exact measurements and placement of the brackets and other parts necessary to hang blinds are of utmost importance. Most manufacturers provide good instructions for the installation of their products, and suggest methods of measuring your windows for the best and most exact fit.

Conventional placement of horizontal Venetian blinds includes: from exterior edges of the frame, side-to-side and top-to-bottom, or within the window casement with an almost exact fit. A single blind can be used to coordinate more than one window, if you will want the same light adjustment at the same time from each window. You can even run blinds ceiling to floor.

Vertical blinds work best in wall-to-wall applications, or to span a wide length of window. They can go from ceiling to floor, window apron, or sill. The wonderful sweeping effect of vertical blinds is lost if you use them for narrow spaces, so think in terms of wide areas. The vertical lines created with these blinds add to the visual height of a room.

Traditional louvered shutters are used in combination with screens so this modern window/sliding door fits in with the traditional furnishing of the room. Top shutters can be opened while bottom shutters are closed to form a visually smaller window area. (Ege Rya "Folklore" rug)

The colorful carpet in this room provides a decorative theme for the solid shutters used at the window. Stylized flowers appear on both front and back of the shutters, and the window is attractive either open or closed. (Viking Anso nylon carpeting by Allied Chemical Corp.)

Shutters

Shutters are often chosen where a rustic effect is desired, especially with the warm look of wood. Within this category are a number of different styles, including shutters with fixed or movable louvers, shutters with panels that will take shirred fabric, and even shutter arrangements that can be used with solid panels. Gay and cheerful, shutters can be effectively combined with café curtains or casual colorful shades.

Preassembled, hinged shutter sets are easiest to install with a slight cutting or frame building for the do-it-yourselfer. Sometimes shutters are left open, used to frame windows for decorative effect. If you plan to use shutters to cover the windows, make sure that they are installed plumb so that they do not swing open unbidden. Window edges, especially in an older home, may need special treatment to provide a plumb edge for installing the shutters.

Shutters painted the same color as the walls offer an interesting yet cohesive effect. Contrasting shutters, either wood-stained or painted, give windows a

character of their own. In either case, choose a shutter style that fits well with the rest of the room, and works well with the window being covered. You will also want to make sure that the shutters do not interfere with the opening and closing of the window itself. For example, louvered shutters would look somewhat busy with a louvered or awning window, while they would look right in character with the more traditional casements, or double-hung sash windows. While these generalities apply, do not be deterred from trying creative window treatments with shutters no matter what your basic window style. A combination of café curtains and shutters can be very striking with even a large-size picture window.

Bare Windows

The bare-window look falls into the category of streamlined decorating. Especially effective with windows of unusual shapes or sizes, or with a wonderful view. The main problem with bare windows is that they can look totally barren and almost scary at night,

Bare window looks depend on rich texture in the rest of the room to soften their impact, especially at night. Here, patterned multicolored rug, and plush pillows, give softness. (Bigelo-Sanford, Inc. carpeting)

draperies, shutters, or shades that comprise the treatment. The key to success is to convey an architectural integrity to whatever window covering you are introducing. It will have that integrity if it goes to a sill, apron, or floor, and is nicely started at the top. If you want your window treatment to extend beyond the window itself, then consider adding an architectural-looking heading or framing that will unify the window covering.

A valance is the most popular of these, and can be used interchangeably for many of the window coverings. Made of either fabric or solid material (the latter often covered with matching curtain fabric), this is a modesty panel that covers the working parts of draperies, blinds, or shades at the top. It gives definition to the overall width of the window treatment. A valance implies windows larger than their actual size, if you are using your window treatment to visually enlarge a window.

Lambrequins. Lambrequins are decorative wooden constructions projecting several inches away

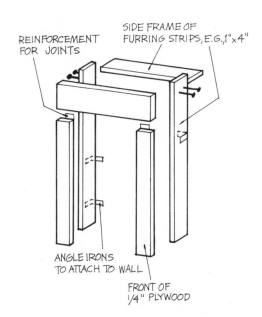

REINFORCEMENT FOR JOINTS

SIDE FRAME OF FURRING STRIPS, E.G., 1"x4"

ANGLE IRONS TO ATTACH TO WALL

FRONT OF 1/4" PLYWOOD

without decoration of some sort. One means of making the most of a bare window treatment is to invest in outdoor lighting so that the same view that is charming during the day is also attractive and magical at night. Another way of handling the night-time block of darkness found with a bare window is to use panels that can be brought across the expanse after dark. These can be covered with an interesting mural or fabric design to give a substitute for the view that has been darkened.

Pay special attention to the frame of any window that you want to leave bare. Hardware should be of best quality, since it will attract the eye more than the same hardware on a decorated window. You may want to emphasize the frame of the window itself, using an accent color. This will give the window a finished look without hindering its basic bareness.

Other Solutions

Giving a finished look to your windows, no matter what the chosen style, is just as important as the

You can make a lambrequin of any proportion, and even shape the inside edges for artful decorative effects. The simplest system is to use furring (usually 1" x 4" for the top and sides), and use ¼" plywood for the front. The front is an inverted "U", supported and attached to the side frames with nails and glue. Cut 2 pieces of furring the height of finished lambrequin, and furring the width of finished lambrequin, minus sides. Glue and then nail sides to top. Cut plywood to cover top (e.g., 12 inches deep) and as wide as frame, and attach to frame top with flue and nails. Then cut plywood for side fronts in length from floor to top (e.g., 6 to 8 inches wide). Attach and reinforce joints from top to side fronts, and side panels to front panels. Attach entire unit to wall with angle braces. Cover with fabric, wrapping it 2 inches to back and stapling in place.

from the wall and framing the top and sides of the window. Width is determined by the space needed when curtains are pulled back, and overall dimensions of the window itself. The simplest way to make one is to measure your window dimensions, cut plywood to size to make the frame, and then staple all around the edges, an inch or so in from the back. Painted or wallpapered lambrequins are also used; if done well they can give the window greater impact on the room design.

Painting. Another means of giving a window treatment a finished look is painting the window frame to coordinate with the window covering. For instance, you might pick up the background color of either café curtains or a decorative printed shade and paint the entire window frame to match. Or, add molding below the window frame to the baseboard, and paint it and enclosed wall to match. The end result is a window that appears to extend to the floor.

Extensions. Panels below windows also can be papered to match shades or drapes. Add some type of border that works with the window frame to give the visual addition substance. Another method is to use café curtains below the window. Then, the real window seems double, since you have created the illusion of additional window below the real one. This technique is especially effective when working with small windows in a basement, either by extending the window treatment to the floor or by creating a false framing below the small window.

Illusions. Window illusions may be the only solution to an almost totally enclosed space, as is often found in basement family rooms. Totally artificial windows can be built in. You will need to install back lighting and an opaque sheet to diffuse the light to simulate sunlight. These are easiest to install in paneled walls that have sufficient depth to accommodate an artificial window. The principle is similar to that of a shadow box, but the window is covered conventionally with semi-transparent curtains or shutters to allow a bit of the artificial sunlight to shine through.

Add to the impact of a small window by using supplementary light with your window treatment. A check with your store will show a range of valance and fluorescent light fixtures that will throw a nice field of light across closed curtains. Safety factors are built into the combination valance/light units, to make sure that hot lights are not placed right next to curtains.

Creating a plant center is another way of seemingly bringing the outdoors into a relatively windowless room. Investigate the units that include the grow lights necessary for healthy plants, plus soft lighting that will enhance the atmosphere. Be sure to provide an additional type of lighting if the grow lights you are using cast an unpleasant hue or intensity.

Super Ceilings

Your ceiling can add spaciousness, light, and good acoustics to your family room. Ceiling treatments vary according to the location you have selected for your family/recreation room. If in the basement, be especially careful to choose colors and ceiling treatments that create an above-ground feeling. Of course, you may want the decorative effects of dark and mysterious paneling or paint, even on the ceiling. But a good rule of thumb is to keep these touches to a minimum, when you are working with a space that by its very nature is secluded and enclosed.

The most popular choices for unfinished ceilings are to enclose the rafters of an unfinished basement with wallboard, or to suspend easily installed tiles.

Before you decide upon the method that is best for you, consider the chances of incorporating interesting and dramatic lighting along with the ceiling. Recessed spotlights, track systems that are suspended along with the ceiling, or recessed lighting panels, such as those designed specifically to coordinate with manufacturer's tiles, are among your options. When decorating an entire room, take care of ceilings first, so that any mess the process creates does not damage walls or floors.

Already-finished Ceilings

Try decorating with paint, paneling, or wall covering. Follow the instructions in wall applications for using these materials, but with these variations.

Paint. Painted ceilings are done across the narrow width. In this way, you can continue painting a new section while the last section is still wet. Start by painting around the borders, then fill in the center.

You can tint a ceiling to match the wall color for a good blend, and still keep a semblance of spaciousness. Ceilings painted exactly the same tone will generally look darker, since they do not have as much light reflected from them. White ceilings look highest of all.

Paneling. Paneled ceilings often are attached with furring strips, using a paneling that matches the walls. The groove pattern of the paneling can add to the width of a room when used in that direction. To achieve a rustic look without the total enclosure of paneling, you can use beams instead. Paneling manufacturers and other wood product suppliers stock these items in both artificial types that are easily glued into place, or actual wood beams that simulate the weathered and rough-hewn pieces often found in barns and older buildings.

Wall Covering. Wall covering on the ceiling is easiest to install along the length of the room, but requires sturdy ladders as well as the help of a friend. The placement and positioning of the strips is similar to placement along the wall; you allow 3 inches on either end to lap down the walls before trimming. Once the ceiling strip is in place, it is trimmed to ½ inch down the wall. This extra edge will then be covered with the wall covering placed on the wall. A very accurate plan is needed for matching patterns from the ceiling down onto the walls. Usually, strips are placed so that they appear to continue directly down from the ceiling to the floor along the longest walls.

Unfinished Ceilings

Paneling and tiling systems are so designed today that a do-it-yourselfer will find them easy to install. And, you can even use the rough unfinished ceiling if you so choose.

Unfinished. Casual unfinished ceilings may have interesting structural parts that lend themselves to exploitation. To disguise unfinished ceilings, paint them in a retiring shade. If drama is part of your plan, choose a color as dark as navy blue or even flat black. Keep in mind that such dark colors will demand additional lighting, since they offer no reflection.

If upbeat contemporary is your style, consider decorating any exposed pipes by painting them bright and cheery colors. Sometimes, making the most of the obvious is the most artistic way of decorating. You also might consider using any exposed beams by staining them or leaving them bleached for a casually unfinished look.

Tiles. Acoustical tiles are good choices if you want to maintain relative calm in the other areas of the house while the family room is in service. These are most often installed in a suspended ceiling system, and are rated according to the amount of sound-deadening insulation they offer. A variety of pattern and texture choices in fire-resistant materials are available, and the systems for installing them are relatively easy to handle.

Check with the manufacturer's accessory pieces for installing any suspended ceiling. Often, the tiles or panels are made to slide into one another, tongue and groove fashion, cleverly anchored on channels that allow for fast layup. The preparation is mainly the layout of the ceiling, which can be accomplished by using the guidelines for laying floor tiles. Once the strips are in place, the tiles are quickly positioned.

This type of ceiling tile shows narrow seams for an overall smooth effect. (Front panel "Turn Oaks Brigantine", side panel "Berkshire Sheffield"; "Salerno" ceiling tile and paneling from U.S. Gypsum Company)

In addition to a wide choice of tile types to suit your decor, there is a choice in the kind of installation that will best suit your needs. If your ceiling is relatively flat and in good condition, you can use adhesive to tile directly to it. The tiles are constructed with a flange that is stapled into the ceiling to hold the tile in place while the adhesive sets up. The next tile covers up the flange, so that the finished job has a smooth look.

Compensating for Defects

When you want optimum in height, but the ceiling is cracked or not level, consider one of the furring channel systems. Pre-formed furring strips are attached first to joists through the existing ceiling, then the panels or tiles are easily attached to their permanent grid system.

To completely hide ceiling obstructions, lower a too-high ceiling, or incorporate recessed lighting directly into the ceiling, consider the real eye-foolers—seemingly solid tiled ceilings that are suspended. The main supports are suspended with wires from the joists and by a wall molding. Planks or tiles are tightly fitted onto the runners and cross tees that make a grid from which they are suspended. Once the job is set up, it looks just as solid as a regular ceiling.

1. Armstrong's Integrid ceiling begins with either metal or wood wall molding nailed at the desired height on all four walls. First, a chalk line is drawn around the perimeter of the room ¾ inches above the intended ceiling height to serve as a guide for molding. Panels are adjusted in length and width around the sides so that partial panels are equal on either end of the room, and full-sized panels are centered.

A lay-in panel suspension system is useful in lowering a too-high ceiling, and allows you to get to any wiring or plumbing by simply moving a panel aside even when installed. (U.S. Gypsum Company)

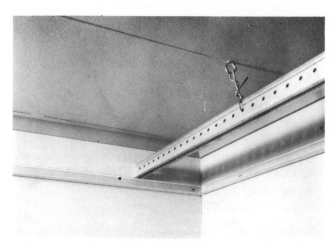

2. Integrid main runners are installed with hanger wires, with the first runner always located 26 inches out from the sidewall and the remaining units placed 48 inches on center, perpendicular to the direction of joists. The system is so simple that it takes no complicated measuring or room layout.

3. Once all main runners are in place, ceiling tiles are installed by starting in one corner. Tile is laid on the molding and a four foot cross-tee is snapped into the main runner. Then the tee is slid into a special concealed slot on the leading edge of the tile.

4. The rest of the ceiling is laid up similarily, with tiles and cross-tees inserted in the same way. All metal suspension hangers are completely concealed as the ceiling goes up.

5. Finished ceiling looks solid.

A lay-in panel suspension system is also used to lower a too-high ceiling or suspend below ceiling obstructions. If yours is an old house and experience shows that you might need to get to the pipes above the ceiling, this is the best choice, since you can easily move the panels. The disadvantage of this system is that the more commercial-looking grid is exposed on the surface of the ceiling.

The proper tools, simple grid systems, and ease of installation of the premeasured and organized tiling systems, make them popular for finishing any family room area.

9. Custom Built-Ins and Quick Ideas for Problem Areas

Much of the fun of creating your own family or recreation room is in personalizing it with your own designs. The really advanced do-it-yourselfer has probably already schemed up a number of additions that can be turned out in the workshop. But even the less-experienced person can create special effects that will be the envy of friends and neighbors alike, and particularly suit the needs of the family in using the room. Here are some of the ways in which you can personalize your family/recreation room.

Built-In Furniture

Built-in furniture takes up less visual and real space than many pieces of manufactured furniture. By building in the furniture yourself, you can gear it to the specific space problems that are unique to your family room. And you can be sure that the design is ideally suited to the activities you want to undertake.

One major advantage of built-in furniture is added, hidden, cleverly disguised storage. It makes little difference what shape the storage takes; it is a rare house that ever has enough.

Modular Units

The modular unit illustrated here can be lifted in total and recreated in your family room. Or you can use whatever components suit your specific situation best. The plan, developed by the Weyerhaeuser Company for *Family Handyman* magazine, looks so professionally finished and compact that it is hard to believe there is so much storage space hidden inside it.

The built-in furniture shown here is the basis for many units that you can adapt for your own family room. Rusticana natural pecan paneling is used throughout, even on the walls. (Paneling by Weyerhaeuser Company)

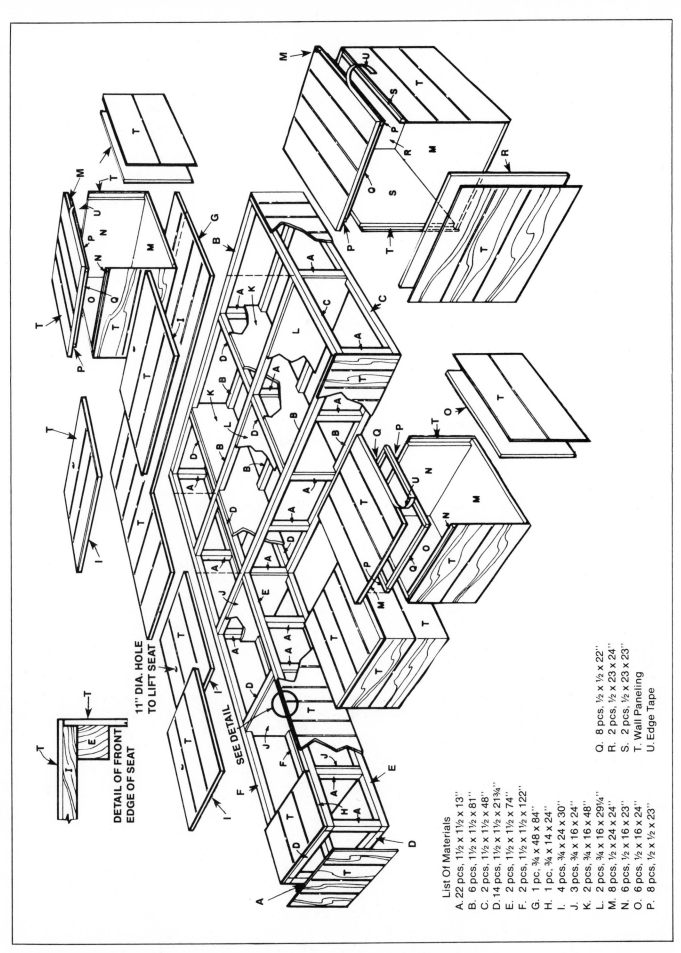

DETAIL OF FRONT
EDGE OF SEAT

11" DIA. HOLE
TO LIFT SEAT

SEE DETAIL

List Of Materials

A. 22 pcs, 1½ x 1½ x 13"
B. 6 pcs, 1½ x 1½ x 81"
C. 2 pcs, 1½ x 1½ x 48"
D. 14 pcs, 1½ x 1½ x 21¾"
E. 2 pcs, 1½ x 1½ x 74"
F. 2 pcs, 1½ x 1½ x 122"
G. 1 pc, ¾ x 48 x 84"
H. 1 pc, ¾ x 14 x 24"
I. 4 pcs, ¾ x 24 x 30"
J. 3 pcs, ¾ x 16 x 24"
K. 2 pcs, ¾ x 16 x 48"
L. 2 pcs, ¾ x 16 x 29¼"
M. 8 pcs, ½ x 24 x 24"
N. 6 pcs, ½ x 16 x 23"
O. 6 pcs, ½ x 16 x 24"
P. 8 pcs, ½ x 1½ x 23"
Q. 8 pcs, ½ x 1½ x 22"
R. 2 pcs, ½ x 23 x 24"
S. 2 pcs, ½ x 23 x 23"
T. Wall Paneling
U. Edge Tape

Cubes and rectangles are the basic forms used for this built-in grouping. Make them to exact size or adapt the designs to the dimensions you need. (Reproduced courtesy of Communications Corp., ©1976, from Family Handyman, Oct. 1976)

Although they have an appearance of substance, the cabinet at the end of the bunk, the coffee table, and the space under the bunk provide hidden storage space. Foam rubber mattresses become casual seating here, but are put to further use for guest sleeping. You can alter the dimensions of these units in creating the sleeping and seating units needed in your family room, but can use the same techniques in designing and building them.

The coffee table is one of the simplest units in this set. It is designed to look like a set of stacked boxes. It is really two large boxes made of ½-inch plywood, and covered with pecan wall paneling fastened to the plywood with panel cement and brads driven through the black scoring. The boxes have mitered corners fastened with glue and reinforced inside with 3-inch right-angle braces.

The covers overlap the sides slightly and are edged with thin strips of wood stained to match the pecan paneling on the covers and sides. There are 1-inch-by-1-inch cleats on the underside of the covers on all four sides, which hold covers firmly in place. The covers are not hinged and are simply lifted to open the boxes. With light objects stored inside, the units are relatively easy to move if necessary.

The cabinet on the left side of the bunk is made in much the same way as the coffee table. Its top can also be lifted for storage. Pillows are placed upright for an attractive display; they become comfortable seating for those using the cabinet or for casual lounging on the floor.

The bunk has a framework of 2 x 2's put together with nails and glue. The front of the bunk is covered with the same pecan paneling and is fastened to the framework with panel cement and colored finishing nails.

The top area of the bunk is made of ¾-inch plywood and also is covered with paneling. The forward edge of the top paneling extends beyond the plywood, and beneath it enough to be flush with the front paneling of the bunk. The edge is painted black to match the random scoring of the paneling.

The top area of the bunk is cut into two sections on both sides of the corner. All four seat sections can be lifted to make use of the storage space beneath them. The sections can be hinged at the back but this means that you have to lift them by the ¼-inch paneling edge in front. This is not advisable since it means conspicuous finger marks and possible chipping of the edge.

To avoid this problem, bore two ¾-inch finger-holes in each section of the top covers at the back, where holes will be concealed by the pillows. The finger holes will permit easy lifting of the sections. To prevent any looseness or movement of these sections, nail cleats to their undersides in the spaces between the 2 x 2's that support the seat sections.

The conventional bunk mattresses are doubled for extra softness here, and to allow for sleeping for two guests with one mattress placed on the floor. Another nice touch is the use of an extra edge along the front of the mattress, where comfortable pillows can be placed. With the warmly covered flooring, this setup is ideal for a family that loves to lounge on the floor itself. Plenty of pillows can be instantly shifted for floor seating, but restacked on the built-in when not in use, for a semblance of organized clutter.

A variation in heights and sizes of the basic cubes of this unit give it an almost landscaped feeling. These various additions coordinate beautifully with the cubed coffee table, and give style to what would be a rather straightforward built-in. Using the same elegant paneling on the walls as is used on the furniture adds to the architectural feeling of the entire unit. A cube one half the size of the coffee table is placed directly on the bunk, while an end cube of greater height gives an unexpected change of pace.

Customizing

Stylizing built-ins can be easily accomplished with the use of trims that match the style of other furniture in your room. Simple squares, rectangles and cubes thus take on a more finished furniture look.

Some of the materials you can use to add personality to built-ins include:

Tiles. Either ceramic, or metallic, or floorcovering, all are easily applied with the mastic that adheres them to walls. For instance, you might cover a storage cube with ceramic tiles in a blue-and-white Delft ship design for a nautically themed family room. Or, combine tiles for a carefree top surface, with stained wood on the sides.

Paint. Try both solids and graphic effects. Simple cubes take on a countrified air with the addition of antique paint and stencils. You might even go a step further and distress the wood by scuffing and marring it. Lacquered looks are also handsome, if your wood is smooth and corners are well finished.

Wall covering. Use covering either matching or contrasting with the rest of the room. Permanent built-ins that are aligned along the walls lend themselves well to matched treatment. Since the built-ins will blend with the walls, they will make the room look larger.

Fabric. For a softened look, you can add quilt backing to give an upholstered appearance to the fronts of built-in bunks before stapling fabric in place around the edges. Cover the staples by gluing on welting or other trim. A more sleek line is created by stapling fab-

Carpeting covers these built-ins and even extends up on the wall. Use a tight pile of carpeting for this sort of application, and one that will hide soiling, such as this "Batik Royale" patterned carpet of Anso-X fiber. (Allied Chemical Corporation)

ric directly to the built-in, or covering it in fabric using wallpaper paste.

Staining and adding furniture hardware. Decorative hardware that is in keeping with the styles used on free-standing pieces, and a stain that simulates the surface treatment of your choice, give a finished look to any built-in piece.

Moldings, alone or with hardware. Use these to dress up undistinguished, free-standing furniture, as well as built-ins.

Once you think of it, there is really no limit to the kind of materials that can be used to personalize and emphasize built-in furniture. The key to making a family room integrating built-ins with other furniture lies in giving special attention to the built-in pieces.

Vertical Storage

While some of your family room needs can be covered with the kind of storage that is beneath furniture pieces, almost every family room also needs to use wall space for storage. Just be sure to anchor your shelving securely. If modular wall units are not your cup of tea, open shelving is really easy to create with wall brackets and shelves.

Open Shelves

Open shelves call for good organization. Your best bet is to choose styles that are adjustable, so that they can grow along with your needs. Then, plan the layout of the shelf arrangement to complement your furniture and the wall space to be covered. A tall, narrow, series of shelves will make a room seem taller, while a broad horizontal treatment of shelves will emphasize the width of a room. Shelves that fill in a relatively square wall section do not appreciably affect the visual dimensions.

Be sure you visually anchor open shelves that do not extend to the floor. Place a piece of furniture beneath them, such as a credenza or chest or storage trunk. Or, use one of the open shelf units that functions as a bar or desk to give substance and weight to the entire arrangement.

Shelf height is best determined by the objects that you plan to use on them. Allow at least 2 inches head room for books to keep them from looking crowded, and for their easy withdrawal. Sculpture and other objects also look best when sufficient space is left around them.

All your family room entertaining needs can be met with solid wood shelves, adjustable with acrylic brackets on solid wood pilasters. (Naomi Gale/Shelves Unlimited)

A shelf system can convert a conventional wall into the focus wall of a family room. Here, a converted attic space makes use of an angled wall for shelving that sets up the entire den atmosphere. Sofas unfold to make beds. (The Simmons Co.)

Plan the distribution of objects on open shelves as carefully as you would the arrangement of a still life. Solid walls of books become uninteresting and fade into the background. More exciting arrangements include space for objects, artfully set off from rows of books with space around them. The heaviest objects belong on the lower shelves, graduating to lighter-looking objects on higher shelves. You can alternate standing books and those placed on their side to give variety to a library corner.

A super storage system starts with decorative shades that conceal each section individually. Some cover windows, while the others cover open areas that have a peg system to accommodate movable shelves. Exercise board and train table both fold up into the wall. (Springmaid sheet fabric on shades, photo from Window Shade Manufacturers Assn.)

Choose shelf styles that coordinate well with your furniture style and that are in keeping with the objects you plan to display. Lightweight objects in a contemporarily styled room might look best on sleek, see-through plastic shelving. In contrast, heavy books and miniature chests might look best in an Early American room, on decoratively bracketed heavy wood shelves.

Prefinished shelving and brackets that coordinate are easiest to work with. You can find styles at many price levels, and adjust the pieces to whatever arrangement best suits your space. If possible, plan a layout of the shelf system on graph paper before committing it to the wall. Sketch the entire wall, and include elements that will affect the overall look of the shelf system as well as furniture placed on the same wall.

Solid attachment to the wall system is absolutely necessary. By taking care with your initial installation, you can use the same shelves for heavy objects either now or later. Screwing brackets directly into wall studs is one method to achieve a solid foundation; others include using molly-bolts for sheetrock, toggle bolts for plaster, or expanding masonry anchors for masonry walls.

Use a level to make sure that the brackets are lined up properly. They need to be plumb on the wall, and aligned so that the shelves will slot into them on the level. Many brackets are designed for the attachment of the top shelf a foot below the top of the bracket, so that the force of the weight is downward instead of outward. This is another good reason for placing heavier objects on lower shelves.

Attractive brackets act as decorative features of the entire wall system, while those that leave something to be desired are best painted or stained to match the background, and visually disappear. If you plan to use brackets on paneled walls, investigate the wood-toned brackets for an invisible look. And, make sure that you anchor the shelving through the paneling and into the wall for a safe installation.

Hidden Shelves

Hidden storage units can take many forms. Some of the simplest methods of enclosing storage shelves are to use either blinds or shades as quick, efficient coverups. These can be installed as part of a bookcase unit, or suspended from the ceiling.

Using window covering materials to disguise storage is most successful when it is coordinated with the real window treatments. This is especially effective in rooms with a minimum of windows, since the artful disguisers used for storage add to the window effect. Even shutters can be coordinated in door sizes and window sizes, so long as the style is similar.

Partitions that give a look of semi-permanence are also good storage vehicles. By setting off one part of the room from another with a shelf partition, you can increase storage possibilities while creating the space divisions you want.

Free-standing partitions are attractive additions to divide rooms, but are not the most practical choice with rambunctious children. A better solution would be the building of a unit that can be securely anchored both top and bottom, untippable and unmovable.

The use of a solid-looking partition allows you to use both sides as a backing for storage units. For instance, you might build a simple frame upon which you can tack peg-board for a workroom or laundry area side, and use a solid particleboard sheet for the side facing the family room. In addition to providing hanging storage for the side room, the front can serve as a "wall" area on which you can hang paintings, or before which you can install a cubed storage unit.

See-through partitions are the best solution where you want to maintain a visual sweep of space. Suspension shelving systems that use tension rods to be anchored to floor and ceiling are an easy means of installing a see-through arrangement.

You might consider a combination of storage units for a see-through arrangement combination. For instance, you can place cabinets or chests back-to-back at the base of the unit, and have open shelving above them. This will give you storage on both sides.

If built-ins or nail-ups or any do-it-yourself projects are not your cup of tea, invest in modular storage units to show off selected objects while hiding others. With sleek textures such as these, add impact to the room with a fluffy, three-dimensional patterned carpet. (Bigelow-Sanford, Inc. Carpet)

Keep in mind that see-through shelves are only effective when they are left relatively bare. And ideally, the items used on them should be attractive from both sides. For this reason, glasses and other objects that are good-looking in the round are often chosen.

Work Wonders with Moldings

Moldings can personalize furniture, built-ins, and walls. Once you learn the relatively easy steps of mitering corners and coping them, you can achieve really

With the wide variety of moldings available, you can tailor your projects exactly. No two jobs in your home need be exactly alike. (Drawings from Western Wood Moulding and Millwork Producers)

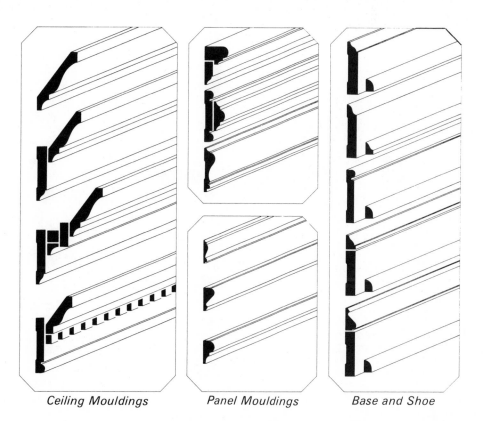

Ceiling Mouldings   Panel Mouldings   Base and Shoe

Molding works wonders in solid colors on plain walls, or used with patterned walls such as these. Plain-jane screens are given a finished look with moldings, too. Frames are painted and then applied to wall with glue or nails. (Western Wood Moulding and Millwork Producers)

Standard patterns

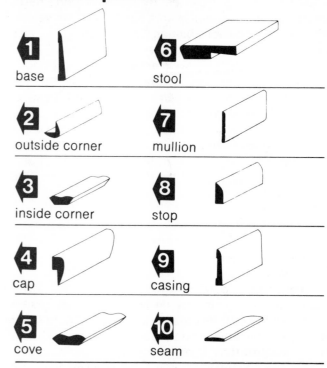

1 base

2 outside corner

3 inside corner

4 cap

5 cove

6 stool

7 mullion

8 stop

9 casing

10 seam

Standard moldings have particular applications, as shown here. Specific shapes are made prefinished and unpainted for job-site finishing. Reproduced from Finding & Fixing the Older Home *by Joseph Scram, a* Successful *book.*

professional-looking results. A molding treatment on your walls can give your family/recreation room a finished look both highly personal and right in keeping with your furniture style.

Making It Yourself

Basic steps in working with moldings require a little practice before going to the specific job. Try out your techniques on scrap pieces before working on moldings you plan to use. You will want to cover these bases.

Materials. These include many already in your tool kit. They are white woodworking glue, finishing nails, a carpenter's rule, coping saw, fine sandpaper, and a miter box and saw. In addition, you will want to construct a jig with the instructions given below.

Mitering and joining. This is the first step in basic molding carpentry. Set the miter box saw at 45-degrees. Trim the ends of the two moldings to be joined at opposite 45-degree angles. When joined, the two pieces form a tight, right angle of 90-degrees. To make corners that are less than 90-degrees, adjust your miter cuts to an angle wider than 45-degrees. For angles wider than 90-degrees (such as those needed for a hexagon), adjust and miter edges to a narrower-than-45-degree angle.

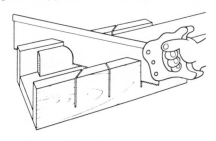

To miter a molding, start by cutting both ends on 45 degree angles in opposite directions.

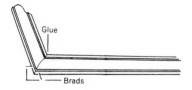

Glue the raw ends of both pieces together and secure the corner with brads.

Coping. Use this shaping method when you want to have one molding butt up to the face of another

molding, instead of being mitered with it. This is often used with cove molding. Coping is also a good method for joining cross-members of a complicated molding panel design, while the corners of the outer edge molding might best be mitered.

You want to transfer the profile of one molding piece to the end of the piece that will butt up to it for a smooth, tight fit. Here are the steps to follow in cutting a right-side coped molding to fit the profile of a left-side butted molding in a corner. (If you want to have the right side butted into the corner and cope the left side molding, reverse these steps.)

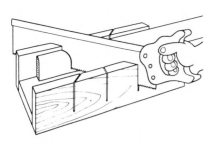

To cope a molding, make a 45 degree cut, angled so that a slanted raw edge shows from the front.

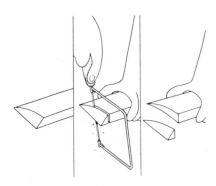

Cut straight back across the molding so that all of the slanted, raw wood is removed.

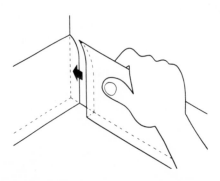

Remaining trimmed molding end will fit snugly to matching molding.

1. Cut left side molding to length with just a square end cut. The coped molding will fit over it, conforming to its outer edge profile. Butt molding into corner.

2. Place matching molding that is to go on the right wall in the miter box, positioned to make a cut in its left end. It is the left end that you will be coping to cover the molding on the left-hand side wall.

3. Prepare to cut right-side molding on a 45-degree angle, going from the right of the 90-degree position. Place molding in the miter box with back upright against miter box backplate. Cut will be on right side in front of molding, left side at back. At this angle the back is longer than the front, so a raw wedge of wood end will show from the front when the angled cut is made.

4. The front edge of this 45-degree cut matches the profile of the left side molding. But, you still have to get rid of the additional raw wedge extending beyond that front edge. Once it is removed, this cut end will fit nicely on the profile of the left-hand molding.

5. Remove raw wedged end by using a coping saw to cut straight back along the line of the front edge. Hold the coping saw at a 90-degree angle from the back of the molding so your cut goes directly across the molding. Once that extra raw wedge is removed, the right molding can be placed so that it butts right up to the left-hand molding.

6. Place your now fitted right-side molding up to the left-side molding. It should match perfectly if your cutting has been accurate.

Making a Jig

A jig enables you to use the techniques of mass production, and is necessary in projects that require "picture framing" techniques of extreme accuracy. A jig is actually a mold in which frames can be made more rapidly, accurately, and with uniformity of size.

The inside dimensions of the jig equal the outside dimensions of the frame. The jig consists of stock pieces of lumber nailed to any flat, nailable surface. Stock lumber "blocks" can be used where necessary to straighten moldings against the sides of the jig. The blocks are cut to the inside dimensions of the frame to be created.

Sides of the jig should be tall enough to give support to the molding, but short enough to allow you to nail into the molding at corners to secure them. Jigs are very useful in creating a series of frames the same size.

Buying Molding

Use forethought, and have a clear idea of the style you want, the design you will be creating, and the total pieces you will need.

Choose a molding style that adapts readily to the design you have in mind, and that suits the furniture style of the room. You will find both unfinished and prefinished moldings stocked, and an almost endless array of types and sizes. Unfinished moldings can be finished almost any way, just as you would finish regular wood. Choices include painting, staining, lacquering. Consider finishing contrasting molding before attaching it, to avoid marking the area on which it is to be placed.

Do not overlook the decorative possibilities of mixing moldings with other moldings or stock lumber, to create very unusual and individual effects. And investigate the prefinished moldings that are specifically designed for use with paneling, with matched easy-care finishes.

In estimating the amount you will need for a given project, the width of the molding should be added to the length for each miter. For example, if a molding is 3 inches wide and requires two miters, add 6 inches and then round off to the amount to the next foot.

It is always wise to purchase all the prefinished molding you will require at the same time to assure a uniform match. And, always buy extra for safe measure. Molding is sold in many lengths, from 3 feet on up, so you do not have to waste much molding if your estimates are accurate.

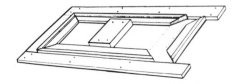

Making a frame to stabilize molding and to allow you to mass produce saves time and assures greater accuracy—it is called a Jig.

Before and after, using sculptured polystyrene ceiling cornices for a touch of elegance. This lightweight material looks like wood once it has been painted, stained, or antiqued. (Photo courtesy of Creative Packaging Corp.)

Installation

Attaching and joining molding is relatively simple. Coped corners and mitered corners are joined with a combination of white wood glue and brads nailed from the outside corners. Make sure nails are counter-sunk below the surface and the holes are covered with a colored putty stick for finished moldings. Use the same countersinking technique to apply moldings to walls and other surfaces. In some cases, colored nails can be used, and counter-sinking and covering is not necessary with nails placed flush to the molding surface.

Projects

Creative molding ideas are included in the illustrations that follow. You can pick up one of these directly, or use any variation of the idea that comes to your own creative mind. It is always best to make a paper layout of any wall that is to be given a molding treatment. You will want to integrate it into the other architectural elements of the wall, such as existing molding, windows, doorways, and any protuberances.

Wall treatments on this and following pages give you some idea of the vase array of decorations you can adapt for your own family room. Use them exactly, or alter them as you wish. (Drawings from the Western Wood Moulding and Millwork Producers)

SCREENS & TRELLIS WORK

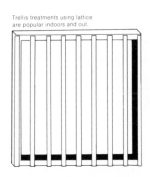

Trellis treatments using lattice
are popular indoors and out.

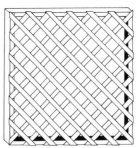

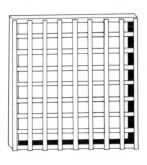

WALL TREATMENTS

Ceiling trim (crown, bed or cove)

Chair rail (traditional height)

Base trim

Wainscot cap or plycap

Plywood, hardboard, or lumber paneling (high wainscot)

Applied moulding for panel look

Traditional wall.

Plate rail wall.

Quarter Round S-4-S

Crown

WALL TREATMENTS

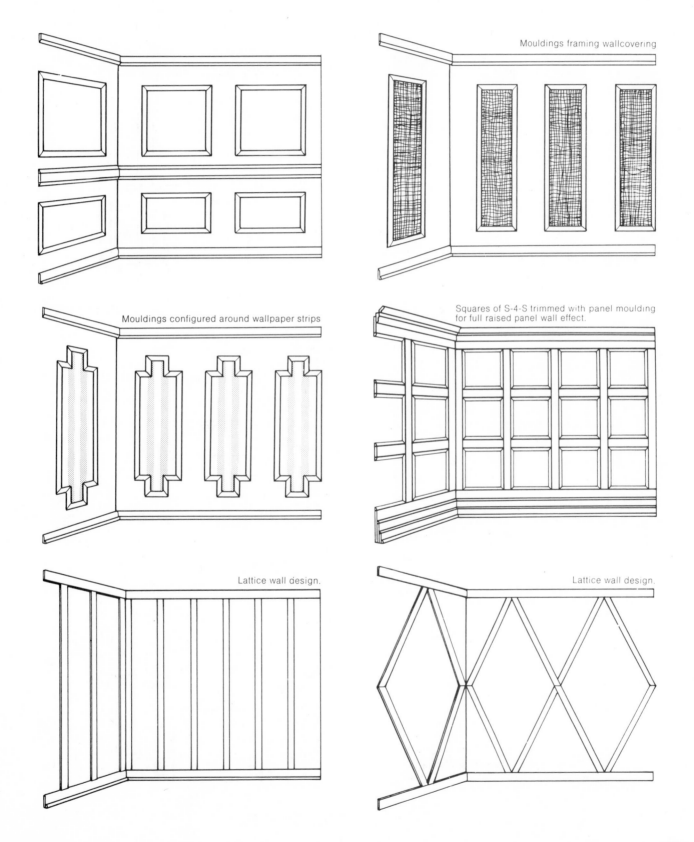

Mouldings framing wallcovering

Mouldings configured around wallpaper strips

Squares of S-4-S trimmed with panel moulding for full raised panel wall effect.

Lattice wall design.

Lattice wall design.

FIREPLACES

Mouldings above fireplace repeat basic mantel design.

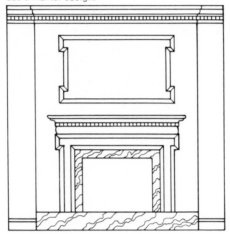

Mouldings used to coordinate fireplace and wall design.

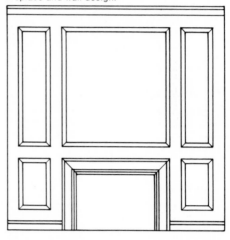

Mantel created with crown moulding and S4S stock.

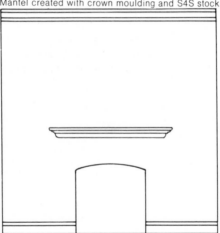

Simple mantel using S4S and crown.

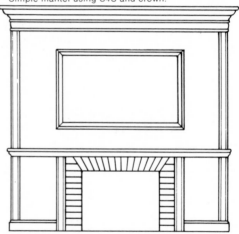

A contemporary fireplace accented by applying moulding in vertical rows.

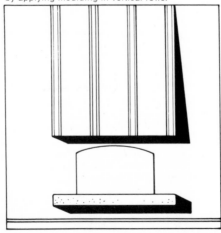

Mantel of S4S and crown coordinates beautifully with applied mouldings and paneling.

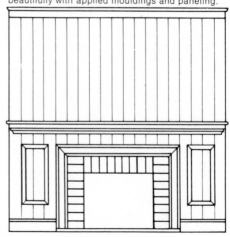

Manufacturers' Addresses

We are grateful to the following companies for providing us with the material on new products for family rooms, and for other related information.

Allied Chemical Corp.—Fibers Division
One Times Square
New York, New York 10036

Aluminum Greenhouses, Inc.
14615 Lorain Ave.
Cleveland, Ohio 44111

American Olean Tile Co.
Lansdale, Pennsylvania 19446

Am-Finn Sauna, Inc.
Haddon Ave. & Line St.
Camden, New Jersey 03103

American Leisure Industries
P.O. Box 63
Deep River, Connecticut 06417

Armstrong Cork Co.
Lancaster, Pennsylvania 17604

Azrock Floor Products
P.O. Box 531
San Antonio, Texas 78292

BarkaLounger Recliners
932 American Mart
666 Lake Shore Drive
Chicago, Illinois 60611

Ther Berkline Corp.
P.O. Box 100
Morristown, Tennessee 37814

Bigelow-Sanford, Inc.
P.O. Box 3089
Greenville, South Carolina 29602

Bilco Company
37 Water Street
New Haven, Connecticut 06505

Bruce Hardwood Flooring Products
E. L. Bruce Co., Inc.
P.O. Box 16902
Memphis, Tennessee 38116

Certain-Teed Products Corp.
Ardmore, Pennsylvania 19003

Chromcraft Furniture
#1 Quality Lane
P.O. Box 126
Senatobia, Mississippi 38668

Collins & Aikman Carpeting
210 Madison Ave.
New York, New York 10016

Congoleum Industries
195 Belgrove Drive
Kearny, New Jersey 07032

Connor Forest Industries
131 W. Thomas St.
Wausau, Wisconsin 54401

Con-Tact Vinyl by Comark Plastics
United Merchants & Manufacturers, Inc.
1407 Broadway
New York, New York 10018

Decorion Division
Stratford Co.
932 American Mart
666 Lake Shore Drive
Chicago, Illinois 60611

Dow Corning Corp.
Midland, Michigan 48640

DuPont Company
Wilmington, Delaware 19898

Ege Rya, Inc.
919 Third Ave.
New York, New York 10022

Ethan Allen, Inc.
Ethan Allen Drive
Danbury, Connecticut 06810

Family Handiman
U.P.D. Communications Corp.
235 E. 45th St.
New York, New York 10036

Fieldcrest
60 West 40th St.
New York, New York 10018

Georgia-Pacific Corp.
900 S. W. Fifth Ave.
Portland, Oregon 97204

Goodyear Tire & Rubber Co.
Akron, Ohio 44316

Heatilator Fireplace Div.
P.O. Box 409
Mt. Pleasant, Iowa 52641

Hoechst Fibers Industries
1515 Broadway
New York, New York 10036

Hotpoint Division
Suite 309
2100 Gardiner Lane
Louisville, Kentucky 40205

Hunter Division
Robbins & Myers, Inc.
2500 Frisco Ave.
Memphis, Tennessee 38114

Imperial Wallcovering
Collins & Aikman
210 Madison Ave.
New York, New York 10016

Interlock Furniture, Inc.
P.O. Box 2188
Waynesboro, Virginia 22980

Intertherm, Inc.
3800 Park Ave.
St. Louis, Missouri 63110

James David, Inc.
128 Weldon Parkway
Maryland Heights, Maryland 63043

Landes Furniture
P.O. Box 2197
Gardena, California 90247

Lord and Burnham Greenhouses
Irvington, New York 14610 or
Des Plaines, Illinois 60018

Majestic Co., Inc.
Huntington, Indiana 46750

Marlite Division
Masonite Corp.
Dover, Ohio 44622

Naomi Gales/Shelves Unlimited
2400 Ryer Ave.
Bronx, New York 10458

New York State Gas and Electric Corp.
Binghamton, New York

Nutone Division
Scovill
Madison and Red Bank Rds.
Cincinnati, Ohio 45227

1001 Decorating Ideas
149 Fifth Ave.
New York, New York 10010

Peters-Revington Furniture
110 N. Washington St.
Delphi, Indiana 46923

Pontiac Furniture Industries, Inc.
Chicago, Illinois

P.P.G. Industries, Inc.
One Gateway Center
Pittsburg, Pennsylvania 15222

Peter Reimuller, The Greenhouseman
P.O. Box 2666
Santa Cruz, California 95060

Shakertown® Corp.
Box 400
Winlock, Washington 98596

Simmons Company
1 Park Ave.
New York, New York 10016

Springs Mills, Inc.
18 W. 40th St.
New York, New York 10010

Stauffer Chemical Co.
Plastics Div.
Westport, Connecticut 06880

The Stiffel Company
North Kingsbury St.
Chicago, Illinois 60610

Stratford Company
932 American Mart
666 Lake Shore Drive
Chicago, Illinois 60611

Sugar Hill Furniture
Lisbon, New Hampshire 03585

Syroco Furniture
Syracuse, New York 13201

Thayer Coggin, Inc.
South Road
High Point, North Carolina 27262

Trend Line Furniture
P.O. Box 188
Hickory, North Carolina 28601

Turner Greenhouses
P.O. Box 1260
Goldsboro, North Carolina 27530

United States Gypsum Co.
101 S. Wacker Drive
Chicago, Illinois 60606

U.S. Plywood
Champion International Corp.
65 Prospect St.
Stamford, Connecticut 06902

Viking Sauna
P.O. Box 6298
San Jose, California 95150

Wallcovering Industry Bureau
Liz King
P.O. Box 503
Mahwah, New Jersey 07430

Western Wood Moulding &
Millwork Producers, Inc.
P.O. Box 25278
1730 S. W. Skyline
Portland, Oregon 97225

Weyerhaeuser Company
P.O. Box 1188
Chesapeake, Virginia 23320

Window Shade Manufacturers Association
230 Park Ave.
New York, New York 10017

Z-Brick Co.
Div. of VMC
2834 N. W. Market Street
Seattle, Washington 98107

Index

Other SUCCESSFUL Books

SUCCESSFUL SPACE SAVING AT HOME. The conquest of inner space in apartments, whether tiny or ample, and homes, inside and out. Storage and built-in possibilities for all living areas, with a special section of illustrated tips from the professional space planners. 8½″ x 11″; 128 pp; over 150 B-W and color photographs and illustrations. $12.00 Cloth. $4.95 Paper.

BOOK OF SUCCESSFUL HOME PLANS. Published in cooperation with Home Planners, Inc.; designs by Richard B. Pollman. A collection of 226 outstanding home plans, plus information on standards and clearances as outlined in HUD's *Manual of Acceptable Practices.* 8½″ x 11″; 192 pp; over 500 illustrations. $12.00 Cloth. $4.95 Paper.

FINDING & FIXING THE OLDER HOME, Schram. Tells how to check for tell-tale signs of damage when looking for homes and how to appraise and finance them. Points out the particular problems found in older homes, with instructions on how to remedy them. 8½″ x 11″; 160 pp; over 200 photographs and illustrations. $12.00 Cloth. $4.95 Paper.

WALL COVERINGS AND DECORATION, Banov. Describes and evaluates different types of papers, fabrics, foils and vinyls, and paneling. Chapters on art selection, principles of design and color. Complete installation instructions for all materials. 8½″ x 11″; 136 pp; over 150 B-W and color photographs and illustrations. $12.00 Cloth. $4.95 Paper.

BOOK OF SUCCESSFUL FIREPLACES, Lytle. How to build, decorate, and use all types of fireplaces. Covers fireplace construction, history, problems, cookery, even how to keep a good fire going. 8½″ x 11″; 104 pp; over 150 B-W and color photographs and illustrations. (Chosen by Popular Science Book Club). $12.00 Cloth. $4.95 Paper.

BOOK OF SUCCESSFUL KITCHENS, Galvin. In-depth information on building, decorating, modernizing, and using kitchens, by the editor of *Kitchen Business* magazine. 8½″ x 11″; 136 pp; over 200 B-W and color photographs and illustrations. $12.00 Cloth. $4.95 Paper.

BOOK OF SUCCESSFUL PAINTING, Banov. Everything about painting any surface, inside or outside. Includes surface preparation, paint selection and application, problems, and color in decorating. "Before dipping brush into paint, a few hours spent with this authoritative guide could head off disaster." —*Publishers Weekly.* 8½″ x 11″; 114 pp; over 150 B-W and color photographs and illustrations. $12.00 Cloth. $4.95 Paper.

BOOK OF SUCCESSFUL BATHROOMS, Schram. Complete guide to remodeling or decorating a bathroom to suit individual needs and tastes. Materials are recommended that have more than one function, need no periodic refinishing, and fit into different budgets. Complete installation instructions. 8½″ x 11″; 128 pp; over 200 B-W and color photographs. (Chosen by Interior Design, Woman's How-to, and Popular Science Book Clubs). $12.00 Cloth. $4.95 Paper.

TOTAL HOME PROTECTION, Miller. How to make your home burglarproof, fireproof, accidentproof, termiteproof, windproof, and lightningproof. With specific instructions and product recommendations. 8½″ x 11″; 124 pp; over 150 photographs and illustrations. (Chosen by McGraw-Hill's Architects Book Club). $12.00 Cloth. $4.95 Paper.

BOOK OF SUCCESSFUL SWIMMING POOLS, Derven and Nichols. Everything the present or would-be pool owner should know, from what kind of pool he can afford and site location, to construction, energy savings, accessories and maintenance and safety. 8½″ x 11″; 128 pp; over 250 B-W and color photographs and illustrations. $12.00 Cloth. $4.95 Paper.

HOW TO BUILD YOUR OWN HOME, Reschke. Construction methods and instructions for wood-frame ranch, one-and-a-half story, two-story, and split level homes, with specific recommendations for materials and products. 8½″ x 11″; 336 pp; over 600 photographs, illustrations, and charts. (Main selection for McGraw-Hill's Engineers Book Club). $14.00 Cloth. $5.95 Paper.

HOW TO CUT YOUR ENERGY BILLS, Derven and Nichols. A homeowner's guide designed not for just the fix-it person, but for everyone. Instructions on how to save money and fuel in all areas—lighting, appliances, insulation, caulking, and much more. If it's on your utility bill, you'll find it here. 8½″ x 11″; 136 pp; over 200 photographs and illustrations. $12.00 Cloth. $4.95 Paper.

Structures Publishing Company   Box 423   Farmington, Michigan 48024